'YE OLDE TOWNSHIPS'

Denby Dale, Scissett, Ingbirchworth, and District
a 'Denby and District' Archive Photograph Album

The author, with his dog, Charis, at Mosley Roughs, Denby Common, looking out across the valley down into Denby Dale in 2006.

'Ye Olde Townships'

Denby Dale, Scissett, Ingbirchworth, and District
a 'Denby and District' Archive Photograph Album

CHRIS HEATH

With Leslie Robinson and Stanley Sheead

Wharncliffe Books

By the same author:

Denebi – Farmstead of the Danes
(Richard Netherwood 1997)

A History of the Denby Dale Pies
(J R Nicholls 1998)

Denby & District – From Prehistory to the Present
(Wharncliffe Books 2001)

Denby & District II – From Landed Lords to Inspired Industrialists
(Wharncliffe Books 2004)

Denby & District III – From Medieval Manuscripts to Modern Memories
(Wharncliffe Books 2006)

'Ye Olde Townships' – Skelmanthorpe, Clayton West, and District
A Denby and District Archive Photograph Album
(Wharncliffe Books 2007)

First Published in Great Britain in 2007 by
Pen & Sword Wharncliffe Books
an imprint of
Pen & Sword Books Ltd
47 Church Street
Barnsley
South Yorkshire
S70 2AS

Copyright © Chris Heath 2007

ISBN: 978-1-84563-043-0

Typeset in 9.5/12pt Palatino by Concept, Huddersfield.

Printed and bound in England by
CPI UK

Pen and Sword Books Ltd incorporates the Imprints of Pen & Sword Aviation, Pen & Sword Maritime, Pen & Sword Military, Wharncliffe Books, Pen & Sword Select, Pen and Sword Military Classics and Leo Cooper.

For a complete list of Pen & Sword titles please contact
PEN & SWORD BOOKS LIMITED
47 Church Street
Barnsley
South Yorkshire
S70 2AS
England
E-mail: enquiries@pen-and-sword.co.uk
Website: www.pen-and-sword.co.uk

Contents

Dedication

To my close family, without whose encouragement and support I would not have the time to embark upon projects such as these. Thanks to them for making sure that other areas of my life keep going.

Also to Shaun and Zara for their unfailing support every time 'Chris' writes another one! Love to you both.

Oh, and thanks to my wife for the title!

Acknowledgements

I have been honoured and privileged to work with two giants of local history I now know that Christmas comes more than once a year – indeed, every time I meet up with them, another 'Pandora's Box' is opened. Between them they have over a hundred years experience in the field of local history research and make my twenty-five seem paltry. They have both been unstintingly generous, kind and friendly, whether it was in Stanley's shed or Leslie's attic, and I can only hope that the trust they have placed in me will be in some way acknowledged by the publication of these books. My grateful thanks to you both.

Stanley Sheead and Leslie Robinson.

Leslie Robinson & Stanley Sheead

Leslie Robinson

Leslie Robinson is the owner of a small textile museum in Skelmanthorpe. This was brought together in order to portray something of the centuries old textile industry, which had, until recent years, flourished in the village – as indeed, it had done in the greater part of the West Riding – but which has now sadly almost disappeared without trace. Emphasis at the museum is centred on the craft of handloom weaving which, almost unbelievably, lingered on in Skelmanthorpe until the 1930's, half a century after it had been discarded in industry. He attributes much of his interest in this subject to his weekly childhood visits to his Grandparents, who lived in Jebson's Fold, Savile Street, Skelmanthorpe, where six hand-looms were regularly at work, two plied by his Uncles. He also has a fine collection of old photographs, which cover many aspects of local village life and events, illustrating graphically the way we once lived, some of which have been used in this publication. All the aforesaid items, along with many others are readily available by the interested on request to him.

The downstairs interior of the Queen Street Museum, Skelmanthorpe.

The upstairs interior of the Queen Street textile museum, showing an original handloom.

Stanley Sheead

Born in Skelmanthorpe in 1927, Stanley was introduced to the values and importance of local history by his Grandfather, Fred Dalton. The interest was encouraged further by the father of his stepmother, the well-known antiquarian and historian, Fred Lawton. Also, the late Tom Wainwright, with whom, for 35 years, they did much research into the history of the village. They formed the Skelmanthorpe Local History Society in 1987, passing on their interest to others. Stanley was also the Chairman of the Huddersfield Society for many years. Stanley spent all his working life in the textile industry and is particularly knowledgeable regarding the history of his former employers, the Field family, one of the main driving forces behind the development of Skelmanthorpe. He helps his good friend, Leslie Robinson, in the Skelmanthorpe textile museum, explaining and demonstrating the mechanics of cloth production with the handloom there.

I must also thank, **Gordon Knowles**, for his contribution to this work. Gordon is a lifelong farmer of Ingbirchworth and belongs to a family that have resided here since at least 1851, when Charles Knowles can be found in the census returns working as a farmer of 14 acres, having moved to the village from Throapham. Married to Cynthia, Gordon has a fantastic knowledge of his district and, being a farmer, of the land itself and the families that lived upon it. He has collected items of local history for many years and contributed to the book, 'The Penistone Scene' published in 1987. It is to him that the section on Ingbirchworth is largely due and he has contributed to other areas. Thanks Gordon.

Finally my thanks go to Nic Whittell and Vivien Teasdale for copies of photographs.

Biltcliffe – Photographers

Joshua Biltcliffe was born around 1852 in Penistone and can be found in the 1881 census returns for the parish living at Prospect Terrace, Thurlstone. Here with his wife, Mary, they raised a family which at this time consisted of three boys, Ernest, John Thomas and Henry. At least one further child, another son, Fred, was born after this. Joshua worked

Joshua Biltcliffe c.1852–1937. (*L. Robinson collection*).

Advertisement taken from the Penistone Almanac. (*L. Robinson collection*).

as a steelworks labourer but had other ambitions for his more creative talents. He founded a photographic shop in a small hut at the Prospect, which prospered and so facilitated a move to grander premises on Bridge Street in Penistone. To supplement his income from photography Joshua also sold violin strings, gramophones and hosiery but it was his studio which gained him the most notoriety. Later he added a picture frame workshop and dark room. Subsequently, further shops were opened in Skelmanthorpe and Denby Dale and he was joined in the family business by two of

John Thomas Biltcliffe c.1880–1964. *(L. Robinson collection).*

Frederick Jubb Biltcliffe 1899–1959. *(S. Sheead collection).*

Fred Biltcliffe's studio in Skelmanthorpe. *(S. Sheead collection).*

his sons, John Thomas and Fred, who, after their fathers death in 1937 aged 85, respectively took over the shops in Penistone and Skelmanthorpe. Joshua Biltcliffe's name was placed on the Roll of Honour at the Memorial Hall, London, by the Congregational Union of England and Wales in June 1937. He had a lifelong connection with Netherfield Church, Penistone – being christened there in 1854, he also held the following offices: Superintendent and Teacher, 1874–1917, Church Member and Deacon since 1886, Church Secretary, 1886–1910, Member of the Choir, 1864–1904, Communion Fund Treasurer, 1918–1937 and Pew Steward, 1889–1915.

Joshua was far sighted and recorded every class at Penistone Grammar school for generations. His son, John Thomas carried on the task recording the pupils, along with his father for a period of around 80 years and Fred made his own mark in and around Skelmanthorpe. Indeed the family recorded so many facets of a now bygone age and their photographs adorn many modern day local history books. They rarely get the credit they deserve for their selfless and farsighted historical preservation. That is not to say that all the photographs in this volume are by their hands, but it would be remiss in the extreme not to pay some kind of recognition to a name which in the Denby and Penistone districts had become synonymous with crystal quality pictures from a time that is now lost but for their work. Their deaths, John Thomas in 1964 aged 84 and Fred in 1959 aged 60 saw the end of both businesses but their names live on through their work.

Most old photographs do not bear a date, we are lucky when one does. In some cases an approximation can be made, but rather than guess at dates to within a decade I have opted to only give them when a date is shown on the original or when they can reasonably be worked out. Many individuals will be able to date some of the photographs, but across this book and its companion volume there are over 800 photographs and sheer logistics currently prevent any further in depth analysis. As a guide to readers, the vast majority of the photographs within these pages date from around 1890 to the beginning of the Second World War, after all – this is an archive photograph album!

Every care has been taken to establish the names of the original copyright holders for the photographs featured within this book and to gain their permission for their use. The author and publishers would like to apologise in advance for any omissions, which will, of course, be credited in any subsequent reprint of this work.

This postcard bears the following statement: *'Ruth E Storer – The Girl Preacher – Denby'*. I would be grateful for any information regarding this young lady and her preaching career. Please contact me via the publishers. *(G. Knowles collection).*

The Townships

Denby Dale

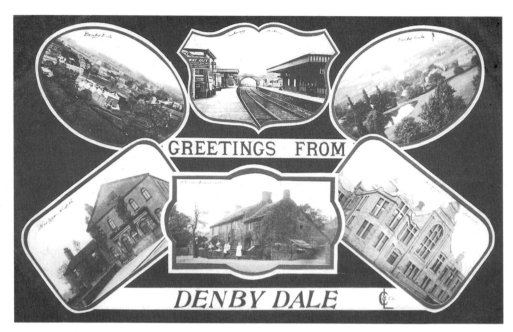

Promotional postcard from the early twentieth century. *(L. Robinson collection).*

Inkerman House, once home to the Peace, Brownhill and Hinchliffe families, on the Kaye-line or Barnsley Road. The gardener, cook and maid pose for the camera. *(S. Sheead collection).*

Denby Dale viewed from behind Kenyon's mill and reservoir, around 1908. *(L. Robinson collection).*

Denby Dale to the East of the viaduct, featuring the clay work manufacturing sites of Messrs. Naylor's and Kitson's and the Wakefield Road going into the village. *(S. Sheead collection).*

Denby Dale to the West of the viaduct, featuring Hartcliffe Mills, owned by the Hinchliffe family. The Hinchliffe family home, Strathdearne and Hartcliffe House. Circa 1906. *(L. Robinson collection).*

A view of Denby Dale from Chapel field, circa 1902. *(L. Robinson collection).*

Denby Dale viaduct, around 1900, a steam train travels along its length. *(L. Robinson collection).*

Denby Dale viaduct, a slightly later view. *(L. Robinson collection).*

The Barnsley Road or Kaye-line, viewed from the top of the viaduct. Hartcliffe Mill is in the centre, Strathdearne is to the right above the mill. *(L. Robinson collection).*

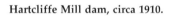

Barnsley Road or Kaye-line, heading towards Toby Wood and Catchbar. *(L. Robinson collection).*

Hartcliffe Mill dam, circa 1910.

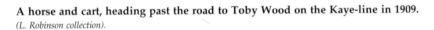

The road to Toby Wood hill top. *(L. Robinson collection).*

A horse and cart, heading past the road to Toby Wood on the Kaye-line in 1909.
(L. Robinson collection).

Rockwood Lodge and gates, Denby Dale. Rockwood House was built by Walter Norton in 1870, he lived here until his death in 1909. *(L. Robinson collection).*

Walter Norton 1833–1909. Walter became a JP, and founded the Rockwood Harriers Hunt in 1868, he kept the hounds at Rockwood House until 1896. He was also one of, if not the, most powerful member of his family's textile manufacturing business at Scissett.

(L. Robinson collection).

The end of the Kaye-line as it approaches the Catchbar in 1922. The gates to Rockwood Lodge can just be seen in the centre. *(L. Robinson collection).*

Carr Bridge, Denby Dale. *(L. Robinson collection).*

Carr Bridge, Denby Dale, 1902.
(L. Robinson collection).

View from the top of the viaduct looking back to Strathdearne. *(L. Robinson collection).*

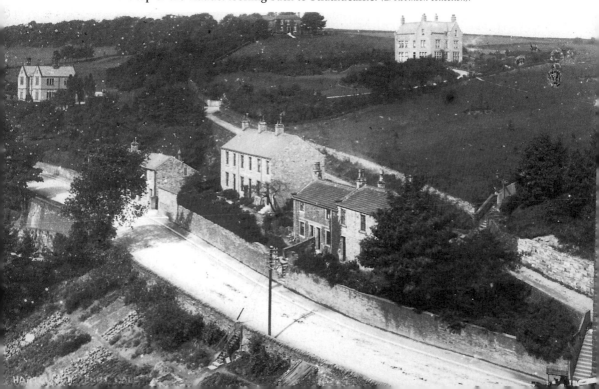

From the top of the viaduct, dated 1903, Hartcliffe Mill is to the left. *(L. Robinson collection).*

Denby Dale station, the viaduct is in the background. *(S. Sheead collection).*

A panoramic view of Denby Dale taken from the top of the viaduct. To the centre, right, an advertisement for Kodak can be seen on the side of the chemist's shop. *(L. Robinson collection)*.

Wakefield Road, heading into the centre of the village. An advert for Brooke Bond tea can be seen on the shop to the left in the now demolished row of three storey houses known as Polygon Terrace. *(L. Robinson collection)*.

Emma Whittell's drapers and milliners(hats) shop on Wakefield Road. Emma can be found here in the trade directories of 1922 and 1936. She was the daughter of Frederick Whittell, one time landlord of the Crown Hotel at Scissett. Emma died on 11 December 1948 aged 74 and was buried at Cumberworth. The shop later became Wilfred Garner's hairdresser's. *(N. Whittell collection).*

Denby Dale village centre around 1900. The People's Stores can be seen to the left, selling, amongst other things, Fry's chocolate and cocoa. Scissett Co.-Operative Society is adjacent to it. The manager and staff posing for the photograph. *(S. Sheead collection).*

Scissett Co.-Operative Society, Branch No. 1, at Denby Dale. Charles Patterson was the manager in 1901 and could well be the man in the apron posing for the photograph. *(S. Sheead collection).*

John Lockwood, the landlord of the White Hart, outside his pub, with his horse and cart. John was reputed to be so strong that he could lift his cart using only brute strength in order for a new wheel to be fitted. John was the landlord from at least 1871 to 1889, though by 1901 Thomas Firth had taken over. *(L. Robinson collection).*

Wakefield Road, just past the village school. *(L. Robinson collection).*

The village in the valley bottom. The old corn mill, Sunny Bank, John Brownhill's mill complex, the White Hart and the Victoria Memorial Hall (built 1903) can all be seen. *(L. Robinson collection).*

A closer view of the latter photograph, showing the Upper Corn Mill buildings complex, dam and Cumberworth Road. *(L. Robinson collection).*

The bottom of Miller Hill, featuring the Upper Corn Mill, in use from at least 1746 though production had halted by 1929. The White Hart pub can be picked out to the top right. Circa 1900. *(L. Robinson collection).*

Above and below. By the early 1970's the upper corn mill buildings had become an eyesore. They had been intermittently used for a number of different enterprises, including a concrete manufacturers. In 1974 the entire complex was demolished. *(S. Sheead collection).*

The Upper Corn Mill, undergoing demolition in 1974. *(S. Sheead collection).*

Corn Mill or 'Millers' Bridge. John Brierley's woollen and cotton dyeing premises can be seen to the right. The row of terraced houses are the backs of the shops opposite the school, which today include an Indian restaurant and an Italian takeaway. *(L. Robinson collection).*

Victoria Terrace, adjacent to the school on Wakefield Road, dated 1906. *(L. Robinson collection).*

Sunny Bank, with Brownhill's mill chimney to the left. *(L. Robinson collection).*

Victoria Terrace, dated 1903. *(L. Robinson collection).*

The Royds, Denby Dale, opposite the cricket ground. Once home to Thomas Albert Hinchliffe (died 1922) and Norman Hall, director of John Brownhill & Co. *(S. Sheead collection).*

View from Millers Bridge, following the course of the River Dearne. John Wood's, later John Brierley's mill buildings are prominent to the left. School lane drops behind the mill buildings at the side of Birkwood House, later to become the Pie Hall, the roof of which can be seen. *(L. Robinson collection).*

A closer view of the now demolished mill buildings of John Brierley, which stood in the area in which the gas holder was later to be built. *(L. Robinson collection).*

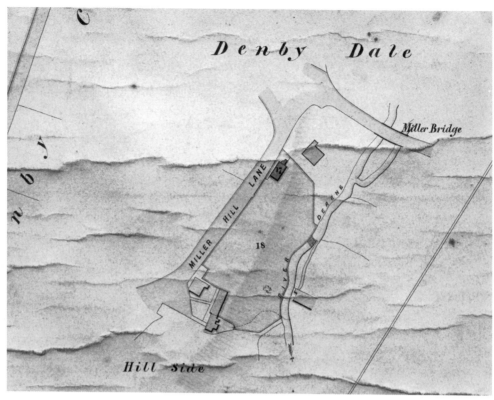

Plan showing 'take off' for John Wood (later Brierley's) mill. *(L. Robinson collection).*

Wakefield Road, to the left is the site of the yet to be built Denby Dale garage, which was demolished in 2006 to make way for new housing. *(L. Robinson collection).*

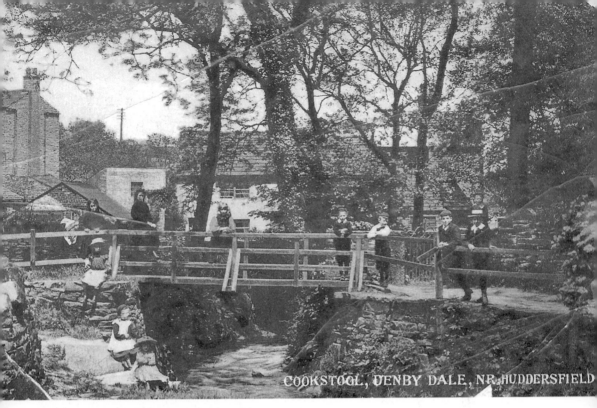

Houses and foot bridge at Cuckstool, 1907. *(L. Robinson collection).*

The Royds stands out in this old view of the village, prior to any building activity at Gilthwaites. The village gas holder and Field House (to the extreme right) can also be seen. *(S. Sheead collection).*

Mrs Senior at Pingle Nook Farm. *(L. Robinson collection).*

Gilthwaites Farm, the building on the left was used for textile production. *(L. Robinson collection).*

This building, built before 1800, was erected purely for the purposes of textile production at Gilthwaites Farm. *(L. Robinson collection).*

Putting Mill, Denby Dale. The photograph shows the old fulling mill, the road to Stubbin House and the colliery road, the lodge pertaining to the Bagden estate and Highfield House. *(L. Robinson collection).*

The site of Lower Putting Mill, first mentioned in 1818, though by 1841 the buildings had become private homes. A document of 1851 relates that there were four cottages, three of which had previously been a fulling mill called Pudding or Putting Mill. *(L. Robinson collection).*

Above and below Mill House at Putting Mill. *(L. Robinson collection).*

Lower Putting Mill. *(L. Robinson collection).*

Part of the scribbling mill at Upper Putting Mill. The ruins of the old engine house can be seen on the left. *(L. Robinson collection).*

Date stone on the scribbling mill, the initials stand for Thomas and Hannah Booth, 1795. *(L. Robinson collection).*

Wesleyan Methodist Chapel on Cumberworth Road. *(L. Robinson collection).*

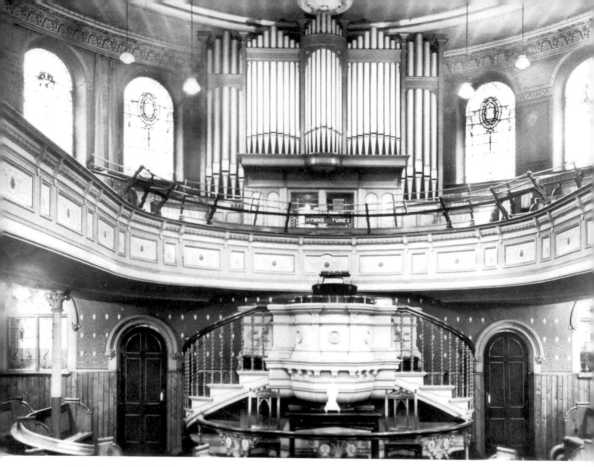

Interior of the Wesleyan Methodist Chapel as re-designed in 1878, before alterations were carried out in 1978. *(S. Sheead collection).*

Wesleyan chapel trip to Wharncliffe Crags, Easter, 1899. *(L. Robinson collection).*

Probably a Wesleyan chapel trip, about to set off from the Victoria Memorial Hall. *(L. Robinson collection).*

Victoria Memorial Hall, built 1903, demolished 1977, photograph dated 1904. *(L. Robinson collection).*

The old 'tin church', and Kenyon's reservoir.
(S. Sheead collection).

The old 'tin church' on Bank Lane, built in 1893. *(L. Robinson collection).*

Miller Hill, Primitive Methodist Chapel, Sunday School, brick laying ceremony, 1st October
1932. *(L. Robinson collection).*

Stone laying at the Wesleyan Reform chapel on Barnsley Road in May 1908. *(L. Robinson collection).*

The assembled crowd at the Wesleyan Reform chapel stone laying, 1908. The building was erected to replace the adjacent chapel which was built in 1860. *(L. Robinson collection).*

Old and new Wesleyan Reform chapels on Barnsley Road. The older building, to the right, was pulled down, after serving as a Sunday school, in 1979.

The Wesleyan Reform chapel, Sunday school scholars, circa 1930.

A large gathering in front of J H Green's grocers and corn merchants. *(L. Robinson collection).*

Above and below. Large gatherings in front of J H Green's grocers and corn merchants. It is likely that the occasion was the visit of General Booth (founder of the Salvation Army) to Denby Dale in 1909. *(L. Robinson collection).*

Mill workers at Jonas Kenyon & Sons, outside the factory in around 1897. *(V Teasdale collection).*

Women weavers at Brownhill's, circa 1900. *(L. Robinson collection).*

Overlooker's at Brownhill's, stood up on the right is Wilfred Haigh.
(L. Robinson collection).

Mill workers at Brownhill's in the back yard. The windows behind the steps are those of the winding room, the doorway led into the packing room. Circa 1940's.

Frances Hinchliffe (with her hands behind her back), stands with the Princess Royal, Princess Mary, at the entrance to the Hinchliffe family home, Strathdearne, in June 1941. The attendant Denby Dale ladies were able to show the Princess the articles that they had made for the war effort. Also included in the photograph is Mrs Algernon Hall, on the front, extreme right. *(S. Sheead collection).*

Denby Dale Council school, class K, with their head teacher, Sam Shepley, who reigned from 1903 to 1934, though he had been at the school as assistant master for some time before his promotion. *(G. Knowles collection).*

Denby Dale Council school, class E, with an unknown teacher. *(L. Robinson collection).*

Denby Dale Council school, class J, with the same unknown female teacher. These last three school photographs appear to have been taken on the same day, the year is unknown, but it was certainly before 1910. *(G. Knowles collection).*

A late nineteenth century photograph of the Denby Dale Brass Band. *(L. Robinson collection).*

Denby Dale Brass Band, in front of the Prospect Hotel in 1889. Left to right: Back row:
F Crossland, H Grayson, S Dalton, J Wood, H Lockwood, A Senior. Middle row: J Pell,
A Dodgson, L Hirst, Charles William Kilner (the landlord of the Prospect), J Hepponstall,
J Senior, C Haigh, F Firth. Seated: J Lockwood, J Pell, J Morley, A Morley, M Pell, A Horner,
W Peace. Conductor – A Morley. *(L. Robinson collection).*

Denby Dale Brass Band, circa 1912, in front of the White Hart, at this time run by John Jewitt. *(L. Robinson collection).*

Denby Dale Brass Band, Charles Kilner (the landlord of the Prospect Hotel) can be seen standing in the centre of the photograph in the bowler hat, circa 1912. *(L. Robinson collection).*

Denby Dale Brass Band, pre First World War. *(L. Robinson collection).*

Denby Dale Brass Band in front of the Prospect Hotel, (now run by Harry Addy) in 1932.
Left to right: Back row: C Booth, F Ward, B Wood, A Crossland, R Haigh, C Horsley, K Wood.
Middle row: C Palace (bells), E Wood, A Crossland, H Cooke, H Morley, V Brown, E Gray,
A Peace, W Lockwood. Front row: J Booth, R Cunningham, F Gill, A Cooke, H Firth, E Crossland,
F Wainwright, F Hudson. The band is shown with their prizes – The Huddersfield and District
Shield and the Crofton Cup. *(L. Robinson collection).*

Denby Dale Brass Band in the band hut in 1935. Left to right: Back row: E Wood, E Gray, W Peace, C Horsley, K Wood, H Morley, W Moorhouse, H Cooke. Middle row: E Crossland, H Firth, A Crossland, F Wood, H Swallow, J Pearson, F Gill, V Brown. Front row: J Booth, F Wainwright, R Gledhill, A Cooke (Bandmaster), H Thorpe (Coach), E Wilkinson, A Peace, R Cunningham, F Hudson. With, left to right – Manchester Gold Cup, Huddersfield & District Shield and the Hospital Cup – Wakefield. *(L. Robinson collection).*

Denby Dale Brass Band. Clifford Horsley is three from the right on the back row. Circa 1930's. *(L. Robinson collection).*

Johnny Garrett, from Kitchenroyd was once a trombone player for Denby Dale Brass Band, he also wrote some of their music. *(L. Robinson collection)*.

'The Surrenderer' and 'Shepley', two pieces of music written by G R Senior of Cliffe House, Denby Dale, which would have been performed by the village band. Shepley was composed in 1912. *(L. Robinson collection)*.

Denby Dale Salvation Army Band, in front of the Wesleyan Methodist Chapel, Denby Dale. Established in 1884, the local corps was only disbanded in 1970. *(L. Robinson collection)*.

Denby Dale Salvation Army Band, circa 1920's. *(L. Robinson collection).*

Cricket Match, Denby Dale, on feast Monday, 1908. *(S. Sheead collection).*

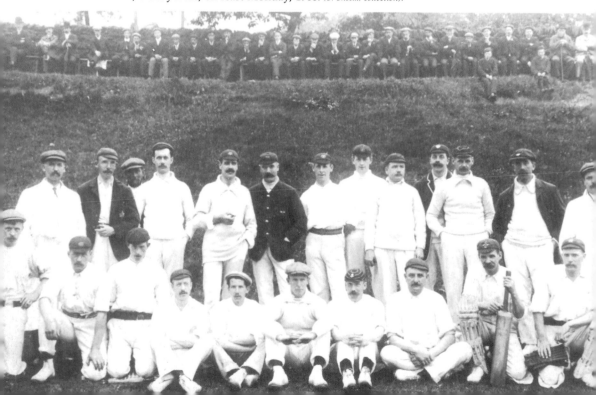

Four members of the Denby Dale cricket team around the turn of the nineteenth century. It is a pity that their names are now forgotten. *(L. Robinson collection).*

The crowd, on feast Monday, 1908, watching the cricket at Denby Dale. *(L. Robinson collection).*

The crowd on feast Monday, 1908, watching the cricket at Denby Dale. *(L. Robinson collection).*

Denby Dale Football Club 1904–5 season, in front of the Prospect Hotel. Left to right: Back row: Garrick Littlewood, Arthur Clay, Joe Jones, Arthur Dransfield, J A Morris, Tommy Brook, Jack Buckley, Sam Holland. Front row: Tom Mallinson, Bill Gibson, John Roebuck, Fred Lockwood, Mickey Barker. *(L. Robinson collection).*

Denby Dale Football Club, pre First World War. Left to right: Back row: George Ed. Exley, Henry Hirst, George Owens, J A Lockwood, Ashleigh Brown, Edwin Lockwood. Middle row: George Sharpe, J G Lockwood, J H Riding. Front row: Joseph H Crossland, Edwin Heeley, Arthur Lockwood, Wilf Dalton, Tom Morris. *(L. Robinson collection).*

Nurses pose for a group photograph whilst working at the First World War convalescent home at the Victoria Memorial Hall, Denby Dale. *(L. Robinson collection).*

Nurses on the steps of the Victoria Memorial Hall, Denby Dale, which was converted into a soldiers convalescent home between 1916 and 1919 to care for casualties of the First World War.
(L. Robinson collection).

Making the crust for the 1928 Denby Dale Pie, in the Salvation Army building.

The 1928 pie dish is finished and ready to use. *(S. Sheead collection).*

The 1928 pie dish on its way to the specially created oven at the corn mill in Denby Dale.
(L. Robinson collection).

The men who created the oven at the corn mill. Pictured above are (in no particular order), Edwin Allot, Joe Noble, Albert Brown, John Hirst, Harry Bedford, Walker Williamson, Arthur Smith, Norman Whiteley, James Ronald Whitwam and Wright Beaumont.

The oven, after 'drawing' the pie.

The pie, as it leaves the oven.

The 'crisis', amidst cries of, '*T' pies bigger than thou thawt,*' the pie is stuck in the oven. After a winch was brought in and men armed with crowbars, jacks and ten foot long tram rails, the pie was persuaded from the oven at the expense of a nearby wall!

The 1928 pie leaves the centre of the village and heads towards the Catchbar on Wakefield Road, after the viaduct.

The 1928 pie procession, lead by the Denby Dale Brass Band, heads back into the village centre.

A close up of the Denby Dale Brass Band in the 1928 procession, themselves being led by a Zulu warrior. *(L. Robinson collection).*

Expectant crowds line the route of the procession. *(L. Robinson collection).*

The 1928 pie being served in Norman Park.

The pie being emptied from its dish in 1928.

Still serving. To the right, one participant shows us his souvenir pie plate.

Revellers throng the trestle tables as pie is still being served.

Denby Dale can be seen in the background as the crowds savour their taste of pie and reflect on a successful day.

The 1964 pie dish is floated on the river outside the Ship Inn at Mirfield as a publicity stunt. Later that day, someone sank the dish! Adding even more publicity to the bandwagon.

THIS CRAFT IS THE DISH IN WHICH THE GREAT DENBY DALE PIE WILL BE BAKED 30,000 PORTIONS OF WHICH WILL BE SOLD ON SEPT. 5TH 1964 IN AID OF CHARITIES

Ingbirchworth

Entering Ingbirchworth village, on the Huddersfield Road from Penistone. The old Rose & Crown Inn can just be seen to the left of the tree in the foreground. *(G. Knowles collection).*

The old Rose & Crown Inn, pictured whilst being run by landlord Thomas Holmes, who was here between at least 1861 and 1904. *(G. Knowles collection).*

The reservoir, authorised by the Barnsley Local Board Act of 1862 and completed in 1868. *(L. Robinson collection).*

The old filter tanks at the reservoir, circa 1920's. Filtering was achieved by using stones, large pebbles and sand, which caused dirt in the water to settle, allowing clean water to run through. Fluoride and chlorine were then added to kill bacteria. *(G. Knowles collection).*

Messrs. Scholley and Town after a successful day's shoot, pictured below the reservoir dam, at the filtration area. *(G. Knowles collection).*

Two members of the Town family with three members of the reservoir maintenance team. William Town was the Waterworks Manager at the reservoir from at least 1869 to 1891. He and his wife, Ann, baptised 13 of their children at Denby church during this time. *(G. Knowles collection).*

School Feast at Ingbirchworth, 1909. *(G. Knowles collection).*

School Feast at Ingbirchworth, 1909. *(G. Knowles collection).*

School Feast at Ingbirchworth, 1913. The tall man in the bowler hat on the mid right of the picture is the wheelwright, Mr Holmes. The man on the extreme right, again in a bowler, is **Benny Beever.** *(G. Knowles collection).*

Coronation celebrations at Ingbirchworth in 1911, for King George V. Edwin Roebuck is the man stood on the extreme right on the picture, with his hands together. It is possible that this photograph was taken by the wall of Denby church, but evidence is inconclusive. *(G. Knowles collection).*

Ingbirchworth Feast, which took place in early July. *(G. Knowles collection).*

Harvest Festival celebrations at Ingbirchworth around the turn of the century. Charles William Knowles is the man in the bowler hat holding the horses' reins. Born in 1868, to Henry Knowles and Mary Hardy, Charles Willie, as he became known, was appointed schools attendance officer at Ingbirchworth in 1897, subsequently becoming registrar of births and deaths in 1903. He was a gentleman farmer and a President of the Farmers Trading Association. *(G. Knowles collection).*

Pre First World War school feast, Ingbirchworth. *(G. Knowles collection).*

Pre First World War school feast, Ingbirchworth. *(G. Knowles collection).*

The Roebuck family, of Ingbirchworth. Back row, left to right: William, Cerilla, Melvin, Turner, Polly, Sarah, Oliver. Front, seated – Edwin, ?, ?, Polly – seated, and Elleanor (Pum). Edwin, born 1877, was the son of Enoch Roebuck, a grocer and draper of Ingbirchworth. *(G. Knowles collection).*

Ingbirchworth Parish Road Surveying Team, outside Green Farm. The cart includes Sam Burdett on the far right, circa 1910.

King George V Jubilee Parade 1935. Edwin Stafford of South View Farm holds the lead horse of his float, his son, James holds the other. *(G. Knowles collection).*

Jubilee Parade, 1935. At the village green, in the paper crown hat is Laurie Beever, Harry Sykes stands next to the man with the darkened face. Edwin Roebuck is to the right of him, in a flat cap. *(G. Knowles collection).*

Denby Band within the Jubilee Parade of 1935 on Fallage Lane. The face of Delariver Burdett Haigh peeps from the left of Eric Turner, the man in a bowler hat, holding a trombone. The man with his hands on his hips is Cam Bus. *(G. Knowles collection).*

Jubilee Parade, 1935. *(G. Knowles collection).*

Float from the Jubilee Parade of 1935. Left to right: Stanley Stafford, Freda Knowles, Marian Stafford, Lorna Walshaw, ?, ?, and the little boy at the end is Gordon Knowles. *(G. Knowles collection).*

Jubilee Parade, 1935. Percy Jackson steadies the horse for the photograph to be taken. Norman Hanson, in the flat cap, watches from behind. *(G. Knowles collection).*

Jubilee Parade, 1935. The Ingfield dray. Alice Jackson is the sailor on the front left of the float, Jean Knowles is between the two male drivers who are Yardley Carnley of Waterhall Farm and William Roebuck. George Cooling steadies 'Flower' the horse. To the extreme right in the dark suit is Henry Knowles. *(G. Knowles collection)*.

Jubilee Prade, 1935. The Broadfield family dray at Ingbirchworth village green. To the left in the white hat is Winifred Jackson, behind her is Nogwyn Jones. Ruth Jones peers over the side of the dray next to her unknown friend. George Jackson is on the right. *(G. Knowles collection)*.

Jubilee Parade, 1935. Left to right, stood: ?, ? Williams, Joan Green. Seated : Jean Knowles, Pauline Wood, Joan Hinchliffe. *(G. Knowles collection).*

Jubilee Parade, 1935. The man seated on the lead dray is Joe Lockwood of Cockle Edge Farm, Ingbirchworth. *(G. Knowles collection).*

Jubilee Parade, 1935. Hand on hip is Kenneth Beever of Ivy Bank, holding the lead pony, 'Sally'. *(G. Knowles collection).*

Jubilee Parade, 1935. *(G. Knowles collection).*

Jubilee Parade, 1935. Harry Sykes is on the extreme left. *(G. Knowles collection).*

Aerial view of Ingfield Farm, Green Farm and the old village green. *(G. Knowles collection).*

Upper and Lower Denby, High Flatts and Birdsedge

King George V, Coronation celebrations, 1911. Though the postcard states that the photograph relates to Ingbirchworth, it seems that it was actually taken outside the gates of Upper Denby church. Bert Town holds the horse on the right of the picture. *(G. Knowles collection).*

Heavy snow on Smithy Hill, Upper Denby in 1933 Milnes Row can be seen in the background.

Two of the oldest cottages in Upper Denby, on Smithy Hill, being demolished in March 1973 after being declared unfit to live in.

The site is cleared and a part of the past is gone forever.

Denby United Silver Prize Band. Circa 1930's. *(G. Knowles collection).*

The George Inn, car park, showing the old stables to the left and the barn at the top of the yard.

Right hand side of the now demolished barn at the George Inn, to the lower left, council houses on the Fairfields estate can be seen.

Denby Park Avenue FC, in front of the George Inn, 1908/9 season. *(L. Robinson collection).*

The Junction Inn, Lower Denby. The left hand cottage is not yet a part of the pub.

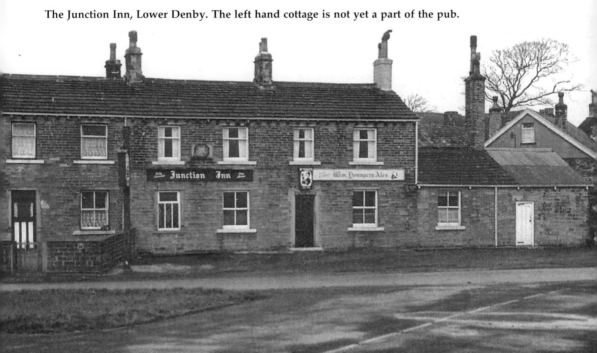

Aerial view of Dryhill Farm and cottages, circa 1950's.

Cottages at the Quaker village, High Flatts. *(L. Robinson collection).*

Quaker village, High Flatts. *(L. Robinson collection).*

The eighteenth century Quaker Meeting House at High Flatts. *(L. Robinson collection).*

The Quaker school house, High Flatts. *(L. Robinson collection).*

Quakers, at High Flatts. *(L. Robinson collection).*

Quakers, at High Flatts, with their band members and choir, circa 1900. *(L. Robinson collection).*

New House, Birdsedge, long associated with the Wood family, who were notable and influential Quakers. *(L. Robinson collection).*

The ruins of Elihu Dickinson's fulling mill at Birdsedge. *(L. Robinson collection).*

The Council school at Birdsedge. *(L. Robinson collection).*

Birdsedge FC, 1927. *(L. Robinson collection).*

Gunthwaite

The old pack horse road, leading from the dam, up to Gunthwaite Hall and onwards to Denby. *(G. Knowles collection).*

Gunthwaite Hall, once home to the Bosville family. *(S. Sheead collection).*

Godfrey Bosville the 4th, 1717–1784, the man who inherited Thorpe Hall, near Bridlington and moved the residence of the family from Gunthwaite, leaving the Hall to be let to tenants.

The old summer house at Gunthwaite Hall, built in 1688.

Cows at Gunthwaite dam, a scene little different from today, illustrating the timeless charm of this hamlet. *(L. Robinson collection).*

The old water wheel at Gunthwaite Mill before the wall was built in front of it. *(L. Robinson collection).*

Steps into the old mill house at Gunthwaite. *(L. Robinson collection).*

Cumberworth

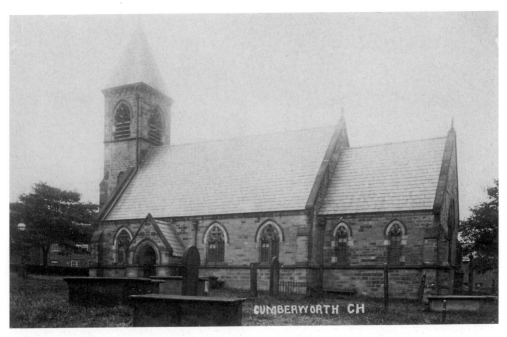

An old view of Cumberworth church. *(L. Robinson collection).*

The Barnsley Road, Upper Cumberworth, heading towards the Sovereign Inn. *(L. Robinson collection).*

O. Haywood's weaving shops. Low Fold, Lower Cumberworth. *(L. Robinson collection).*

Cumberworth Primitive Methodist Chapel Sunday school, under construction at a cost of £700. Work was completed in 1908. The chapel itself was built in 1853. *(L. Robinson collection).*

Knurr and Spell match taking place at Cumberworth, between, on the left, Johnny Lockwood and on the right, Elderman Armitage. *(L. Robinson collection).*

Laying new turf at the cricket ground, circa 1920. Left to right: Jimmy Pell (with pony and cart), Charlie Lockwood (on cart) along with Charlie Allsop. Then right to left: Walter Dearnley, Herman Lockwood (standing), Lewis Tarbatt (Senior), Arthur Kilner, Edgar Peace.

Cumberworth Foresters AFC 1911–12. Back: the landlord of the Forestoers, Charlie Lockwood. Back row, left to right: Hermann Lockwood (trainer), Charlie Allsop, Clement Senior, Clarence Booth. Middle row: Oliver Noble, Ernest Allsop, George William Stephenson. Front row: George Allsop, John Simpson, Dick Senior, Charlie Lockwood, Reggie Booth. *(L. Robinson collection).*

Scissett

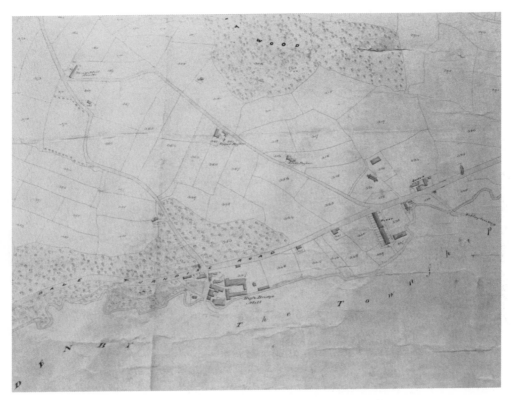

Plan of Scissett as it existed in 1842. *(S. Sheead collection).*

Scissett, dominated by the mill buildings of the Norton family, 1910. *(L. Robinson collection).*

A close up of the Norton family's mill complex, 1910. *(L. Robinson collection).*

Scissett, the village as it was in 1910, showing the church and Fleet Row. *(L. Robinson collection).*

Scissett, the village viewed in 1910. *(L. Robinson collection).*

Scissett, a general view looking on towards Clayton West. *(L. Robinson collection).*

A very old photograph of Kitchenroyd and the Pell family, looking towards Scissett.
(L. Robinson collection).

Lower Bagden Farm. *(L. Robinson collection).*

Datestone on the inside right hand gable of Lower Bagden Farm, showing that it was once on the outside. The letter 'C' stands for the Clayton family, dated 16?? (seventeenth century). *(L. Robinson collection).*

Datestone over a door at Clough House Cottages. The 'E' most probably, stands for Exley, the family name which is remembered at nearby Exley Gate. *(L. Robinson collection).*

Clough House Cottages. *(L. Robinson collection).*

ZigZag bridge, Bagden Drive can be seen in the background. *(L. Robinson collection).*

Bagden Wood at the bottom of Hay Royds. *(L. Robinson collection).*

Highwood Lodge, Kitchenroyd. *(L. Robinson collection).*

General view of Bagden, with Bagden Hall to the centre left. *(L. Robinson collection).*

Bagden Hall, with Stoney Lane in the foreground. *(L. Robinson collection).*

Bagden Hall, an early twentieth century view. *(L. Robinson collection).*

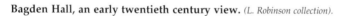

Bagden Hall, an early twentieth century view. *(L. Robinson collection).*

The boating lake at Bagden Hall. *(S Sheead collection).*

The boating lake at Bagden Hall. *(S. Sheead collection).*

Thomas Norton and the founder of the Salvation Army, General Booth, outside the front door of Bagden Hall in 1909. The chauffeur, in the white coat waits patiently before taking General Booth to Denby Dale. *(S. Sheead collection).*

Thomas Norton with his wife, Jessie Jane, seated on the right, outside Bagden Hall circa 1916. The lady to Mr Norton's left was the matron at the Military hospital set up during the First World War at Denby Dale. *(S Sheead collection).*

Thomas Norton (right) in front of Bagden Hall by the boating lake, accompanied by Mr and Mrs G Young, circa 1910. *(S. Sheead collection).*

Thomas Norton and his wife Jessie Jane in the grounds of Bagden Hall, circa 1920's. *(S. Sheead collection).*

Alice Mabel Race Norton 1878–1962, daughter of Thomas Norton and his first wife, Alice Ada, pictured around 1890. *(S. Sheead collection).*

Doctor Duncan Alistair MacGregor at Bagden Hall. He was the first Medical Officer of Health for the district, appointed in 1878. Dr. MacGregor was born in 1858 in Scotland and gained his MBCM at Edinburgh University. He is recorded in the 1881 Census returns living at Scott Hill, Clayton West as head of the household which included his sisters, Janet and Margaret and his brother, Alistair, who was following in his elder brothers footsteps as a student of medicine at Edinburgh. Dr. MacGregor eventually retired and moved to Exmouth, where he died in 1925 **aged 67.** *(S. Sheead collection).*

Highbridge Lane, circa 1940's. *(L. Robinson collection).*

Highbridge Lane, circa 1940's. *(L. Robinson collection).*

Nortonthorpe Mills and Cuttlehurst, from Highbridge Lane, showing J K Whittell's shop.
(L. Robinson collection).

Highbridge Mill House, Cuttlehurst. *(L. Robinson collection).*

Highbridge Mill House, note the tar barrels, ready and waiting to be used to repair the road.
(L. Robinson collection).

Coach house and stable at Cuttlehurst, belonging to Benjamin Norton. *(L. Robinson collection).*

Cuttlehurst, Scissett. *(L. Robinson collection).*

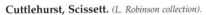

Wilford Kaye's new house at Cuttlehurst 'Cuttlehurst Villa', in 1910. *(L. Robinson collection).*

Wakefield Road, entering Scissett, circa 1950's. *(L. Robinson collection).*

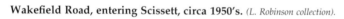

Wakefield Road, Scissett, circa 1950's. *(L. Robinson collection).*

Busker Lane, Scissett. *(L. Robinson collection).*

Four views of the original Lower Busker Farm. The datestone records William Oxley in the 1680's. *(L. Robinson collection).*

Upper Busker Farm, now called Lady Royd and much altered. The date stone was brought from Manor Farm, Skelmanthorpe and records William Oxley, 1710. *(L. Robinson collection).*

Busker Lane. *(L. Robinson collection).*

The Lodge at Nortonthorpe Hall, the two children are Maggie and Leo Finnie. *(L. Robinson collection).*

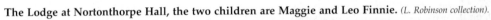

The Lodge, Nortonthorpe Hall. *(L. Robinson collection).*

Busker Lane, the right hand turn leads on to Church Terrace. *(L. Robinson collection).*

The old Barhouse cottages and privys, opposite Highbridge Lane, where the toll bar on the Wakefield Turnpike road used to stand. Its removal facilitated the widening of the junction of **Highbridge Lane.** *(L. Robinson collection).*

Three pubs and Wright's drugstore. Left to right, the Crown, the Queens Head, the British Queen. *(L. Robinson collection).*

The same view as the latter photograph, this time trimmed up in order to celebrate the Coronation of King Edward VII in 1901. Under the banner reading 'Long Live the King' the first Post Office in Scissett can be seen. *(L. Robinson collection).*

Looking back on the previous two views. Ernest Whittle's draper's shop is to the left, followed by the Queens Head, the British Queen and then the mill buildings of the Norton family. *(L. Robinson collection).*

7 Wakefield Road

I. Wray,
P.O. Scissett

The Crown Hotel, Scissett. The man standing in the pub doorway is the landlord, Johnny Peace, circa 1932. *(L. Robinson collection).*

Crown Street, looking down, at the side of the Crown Hotel. *(L. Robinson collection).*

Frederick Whittle, landlord of the Crown, and his family outside the pub, circa 1890. Frederick was the brother of Henry Augustine Whittle who had run the Crown before him. Frederick's daughter, Emma, went on to run a draper's and milliner's shop in Denby Dale. *(N. Whittell collection).*

Scissett, circa 1890. At the bottom left the lattice bridge for carrying coal tubs from Nortonthorpe colliery (trapeze pit) to the coal chute's at the bottom of Stanhope Street can be seen. The market place is still an open space at this time. The four new houses at the top of Market Street were built in 1887 at a cost of £335. *(L. Robinson collection).*

Scissett, created by the Norton family during the nineteenth century, pictured around 1900. *(L. Robinson collection).*

Scissett, circa 1910. The picture is dominated by Fleet Street, to the lower centre, which was built in 1830. Its occupants in 1830 were (from the top of the street downward): William Tyas, William Dawson, Joshua Radley, David Pell, Jonathan Mann, Joseph Whitley, Joseph Woodhead, Thomas Whitley, William Smith, John Whitley, James Doughty, John Turton, David Beever, John Firth. The rent was £4 4s per annum. Stanhope Street can be seen running to the left of the back to back terraces, its occupants in 1830 were, from the top of street downwards: William Hellewell, Joseph Blackburn, John Blackburn, Amos Hirst, George Scholefield, Joshua Naylor, Henry Firth, Michael Barraclough, John Hirst, Frederick Swift, Charles Pell, Joseph Bates, William Bates, George Dyson. *(L. Robinson collection).*

Scissett, circa 1910. The church, Fleet Street and the mill dam for Marshall Mill can all be seen. *(L. Robinson collection).*

Fleet Street, Scissett, demolished in 1938. Its final tenants were (from the top of the street downward): Willie Pell, Old Butchers Shop (built in garden of number 1), Jim Firth (fish & chip shop in garden), Henry Firth, Norman Shaw, Ezra England, Joseph Henry Wood, George H Newton, William Robinson, Irvin Wood, Albert A Tolhurst, Frank Robinson, Wilfred Hudson, Martha Ann Flack Firth (from 1918 onwards the itinerant dentist attended here every Friday from 11:30am to 2:30pm for extractions, the price – without cocaine was 6d, with cocaine 2s 6d.), Annie England. Stanhope Street 1938 (prior to demolition) – from the top of the street downwards: Edgar Exley & Ernest Hobson (joint tenancy), Emma Craven, George Arthur Dawson, John Henry England, Fred Firth, Laura Fisher, Eva Robinson, Albert Robinson, Arthur Craven, Allin Exley, Sam Atkinson, Herbert Tinker, Arthur Batty, Fred Smith. *(L. Robinson collection).*

The landscape after the removal of the Fleet and Stanhope Street after 1938. *(L. Robinson collection).*

A group of 'Brickyard' children, in 1924 'Brickyard' was a part of Union Street: Left to right, back row: Kathleen Wainwright, Nita Wainwright, Dorothy Senior, Nellie Senior, Alice Senior, Polly Batty. Front row: Marjorie Wainwright, Emily Firth, Freda Batty, Kenneth Brooke, Phyllis Sykes. *(L. Robinson collection).*

Houses in brickyard and Ings Dyke Side, empty and ready for demolition during the 1960's. *(L. Robinson collection).*

Crown Street, looking up towards Wakefield Road. *(L. Robinson collection).*

Union Street. *(L. Robinson collection).*

Brickyard houses, empty and ready for demolition during the 1960's. *(L. Robinson collection).*

Demolishing Union Street, 1960's.
(L. Robinson collection).

Wakefield Road, Joseph Birkenshaw's butchers shop is in the centre. John William Jagger's barbers shop is to the extreme right. Photograph taken prior to World War One.
(L. Robinson collection).

Wakefield Road, Joseph Birkenshaw's butchers shop can be seen below Samuel Sheard's green grocers shop, which later became a garage. *(L. Robinson collection).*

Wakefield Road, mid twentieth century. Sheard's green grocers has by now become a garage.
(L. Robinson collection).

To the right, Charles Burhouse's shop, Scissett around the turn of the nineteenth century.
(L. Robinson collection).

C. BURHOUSE,
THE PEOPLE'S
Drapery & Grocery Stores,
Corn Merchant.

DOG BISCUITS.   CIGAR IMPORTER.
BEDSTEADS . . .
WRINGING MACHINES.
House FURNISHER
Market Street, Scissett.

HATS, CAPS AND BOOTS
IN NEWEST STYLES.
Suits to Measure & Ready Made.
ALL NEW DESIGNS.
Try our Noted 2s. Tea.
FAMILY ORDERS PROMPTLY ATTENDED TO.

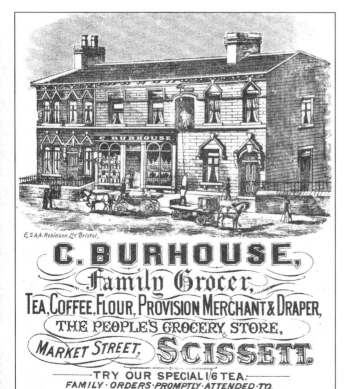

E. S. & A. Robinson, L^{td} Bristol,

C. BURHOUSE,
Family Grocer,
TEA, COFFEE, FLOUR, PROVISION MERCHANT & DRAPER,
THE PEOPLE'S GROCERY STORE,
MARKET STREET, SCISSETT.
TRY OUR SPECIAL 1/6 TEA.
FAMILY · ORDERS · PROMPTLY · ATTENDED · TO.

Top left: Advertisement for Burhouse's general store. (*L. Robinson collection*).

Top right: Charles Burhouse, founder of the shop, who passed the business on to his son, J W Burhouse who was in charge by at least 1912. (*L. Robinson collection*).

Left: A butter wrapper, specially printed for Burhouse's general store. (*L. Robinson collection*).

Wray's newsagents and Post Office, decorated for the 1937 Coronation of George VI. Mary Ann Wray was noted to be the proprietor in 1936. *(L. Robinson collection).*

Wray's shop and Post Office, 1921. The woman in the shop doorway is Polly Wray, the little girl is Margaret Robinson and the dog was called 'Uka'. Lloyd George is featured on the poster. 'Robs' shop (the garage) can be determined by the Mobiloil and BP signs. *(L. Robinson collection).*

The Co-Op butchers, cobblers and main stores. In the Co-Op doorway, PC Ibbotson talks to Jonas Woodhead, the Co-Op manager, circa 1910. *(L. Robinson collection).*

From left to right, the Co-Op main store, cobblers shop, butchers shop and Infants School. The three men stood talking are J Woodhead (grocer), Walter Bentley (butcher) and John Ellis ('Cobbler' John), circa 1905. *(L. Robinson collection).*

Scissett Co-Op, with the Co-Op butchers department to the right. *(L. Robinson collection).*

Co-Op stores, Scissett. *(L. Robinson collection).*

Scissett Co-Op butchers department circa 1930. Left to right: Back row: George Taylor, Norman Tyas, Tom Exley, George Lee. Front row: Irvin Green, Frank Morley, Owen White.
(L. Robinson collection).

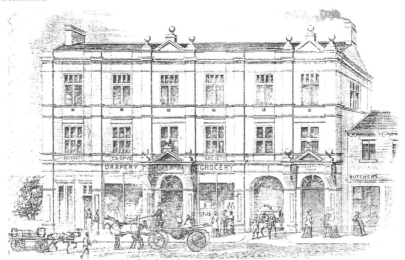

Printed bags for the opening of the Scissett branch of the Co-Op in 1888.
(L. Robinson collection).

Scissett Co-Op butchers shop circa 1925. Left to right are: Norman Tyas (Manager), Irvin Green, Frank Morley. *(L. Robinson collection).*

Scissett Co-Op Mannequin Parade. Centre – Kathleen Barron. Left to right around her are: Stella Schofield, Christine Charlesworth, Auriel Stevenson, Joan Clarkson, Jean Micklethwaite, Molly Wray, Elizabeth Charlesworth, Rosemary Charlesworth. *(L. Robinson collection).*

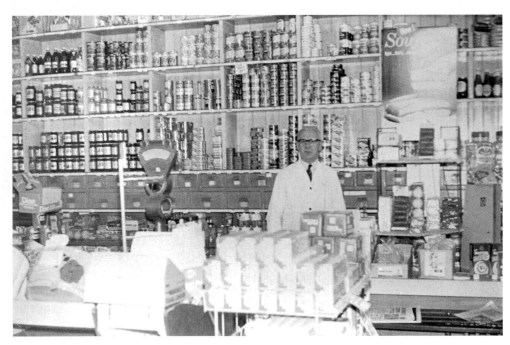

Edward 'Teddy' Higson – the last manager of the Scissett Co-Op, inside the main store which closed on 20 August 1968. The butchers department closed 31 December 1976 and total closure occurred in September 1978. *(L. Robinson collection).*

Scissett Co-Op Mannequin Parade at the Assembly Rooms. Left to right: Molly Dyson, Molly Dearnley, Jean Micklethwaite, Margaret Tinker, Christine Charlesworth, Mrs C Shaw. In front is Stella Schofield. *(L. Robinson collection).*

Wakefield Road, on the left is the Co-Op building. On the right is Dearne Farm House, the telephone exchange (formerly the Carter brothers shop) and the Conservative Club, circa 1900. *(L. Robinson collection).*

Barnsley and Wakefield Road's corner, the man with the cash bag, waiting at the steps of the bank, is Willie Senior. *(L. Robinson collection).*

Barnsley and Wakefield Roads Corner

I. Wray,

Wakefield Road, Scissett, showing the Post Office, up the railed steps and Morton's shop in the centre of the photograph. *(L. Robinson collection).*

Tyas's jeweller's shop on Wakefield Road, circa 1905. Fred Tyas stands in the shop doorway with his wife and his son, Alfred. The local children in the baker's shop, to the left, are members of the Lodge family. *(L. Robinson collection).*

Dearne Terrace, Scissett. The modern day fish and chip shop premises can be instantly recognised to the left. *(L. Robinson collection).*

Morton's first shop was at a house at the end of Dearne Terrace, the premises were later used by Lizzie Brierley as a sweet shop. *(L. Robinson collection).*

Above and below, buildings at Marshall Mill, which was mentioned in the Skelmanthorpe Court Baron of 1653 but which dated back to the medieval period. The miller from 1757 until his death in 1774 was John Horn, in his will he left the tenancy to his wife, Elizabeth and on her death it was to pass to Wheetman Dickinson, *'my nephew who at present lives with me and is my servant'*. Wheetman (1744–1817) married Mary Armitage and had 12 children, one of whom, Isaac (1783–1861) took over from his father. Isaac married Elizabeth Hammerton and was succeeded as miller by his son Weetman Dickinson (1809–1855). Weetman married Eliza Waites and in 1836 they had a daughter, Sarah (1836–1911), who went on to marry George Pearson. Their son, Weetman Dickinson Pearson, became a very successful builder and the First Viscount Cowdray. The Weetman name has been carried on to the present day and the Fourth Viscount is Michael Orlando Weetman Pearson.

Marshall Mill. The Dickinson family remained here as tenants until the mill closed in 1919. The final remaining buildings on the site were eventually demolished in 1940. *(L. Robinson collection).*

Wakefield Road, Scissett, showing the Church and Vicarage and Dearne Farm. *(L. Robinson collection).*

Dearne Farm, Scissett. *(L. Robinson collection).*

Wakefield Road, Scissett, circa 1900. *(L. Robinson collection).*

Wakefield Road, Scissett, circa 1900. Thickett's buildings can be seen, also the gates to Joseph Kaye's rope and twine mill. *(L. Robinson collection).*

Fields, upon which the 'Pennine' estate was about to be built. Digging out began in 1968.
(L. Robinson collection).

Scissett swimming baths, which were regularly used for dances in the mid twentieth century, the pool being covered by a wooden floor. The provision of a swimming and slipper bath was proposed in 1922 as a joint venture to be sited in Scissett with the help and co-operation of the Miners Welfare. The manager of the 'Clayton West and Emley Miners Welfare Baths' in 1936 was Joseph William Bell. *(L. Robinson collection).*

The swimming pool covered by a temporary wooden dance floor. *(L. Robinson collection).*

The Dickinson's family home, Wheatley Hill. *(L. Robinson collection).*

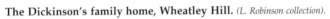

Deffer Nook, Toppit. *(L. Robinson collection).*

The house and shop of William Carter, grocer and provision dealer in Carter Fold (now demolished). William and John Carter were weavers and farmers before the construction of Fleet Row in 1830. As they were already producing the usual dairy goods, the brothers capitalised on their proximity to the houses by altering their livings to that of shopkeepers. William became a grocer and John, a butcher. They later built new premises which continued in business until the arrival of the Co-Op stores across the road in 1888. *(L. Robinson collection).*

St Augustine's Church, Scissett. Built in 1839, largely down to the efforts of local manufacturer, Joseph Norton. *(L. Robinson collection).*

Christmas services at St Augustine's, around 1900. *(S. Sheead collection).*

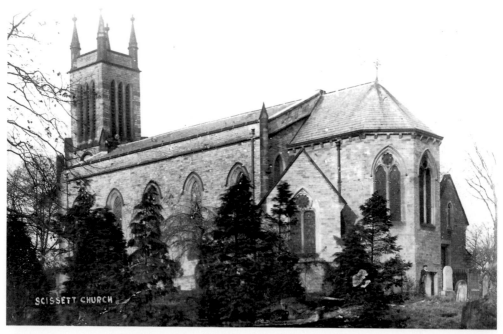

St Augustine's, showing the pinnacles on the western tower, which contained one bell and the apsidal chancel, built in 1881. *(L. Robinson collection).*

Interior of St Augustine's church. In 1881 the nave was thoroughly restored and a chancel built costing £2085, providing seats for 400 people. *(L. Robinson collection).*

Scissett Vicarage. *(L. Robinson collection).*

The school from Dearne Royd. New Laithe cottages stand behind and Marshall Mill in between.
(L. Robinson collection).

Church Terrace, off Busker Lane. *(L. Robinson collection).*

St Augustine's Church – Bible Class, circa 1930. Left to right: Back row: F Ashton, D Robinson, F Armitage. Middle row: L Hardcastle, S Armitage, F Craven. Front row: L Gunson, R Hill, E Craven, E Robinson, A Wood. *(L. Robinson collection).*

St Augustine's Church Parish Tea (men's effort), circa 1930. Back row: G Barraclough, A Wood, L Hardcastle, A Wood. 2nd row: F Armitage, S Armitage, R Hill, H Beardsell, D Robinson, B Dickinson, A Hardcastle, L Hardcastle. 3rd row: F Battye, G W Wray, T Hellewell, E Wray, F Craven, S Wray, F Craven, H Craven, A Dawson. Front row: H Hollingworth, H Peace, C Blackburn, E Craven, E Robinson. *(L. Robinson collection).*

St Augustine's Church 'Brambles Club'. Back row: ?, Parson Libbey, E Craven. Middle row: M Buckley, ?, L Hardcastle, G Barraclough, S Armitage, N Littlewood. Front row: C Mitchell, ?, H Carter, A Mitchell. *(L. Robinson collection).*

Scissett Mother's Union, before 1918, outside St Augustine's Church. *(L. Robinson collection).*

Looking back towards Scissett from the National School. *(L. Robinson collection).*

Scissett New National School, built in 1861. *(L. Robinson collection).*

Morton's new shop, around 1900, just after the turn off for the Barnsley Road, heading towards Wakefield. From left: Emma Jane Morton, Mrs Henry Morton, Elsie Morton, Emily Morton, Henry Morton, ?, George ?, Samuel Morton, ?, Mary Morton. *(L. Robinson collection).*

The china counter inside Morton's shop. Leslie Robinson has counted 532 pieces of crockery in the photograph. *(L. Robinson collection).*

Morton's shop, on Wakefield Road, circa 1900. *(L. Robinson collection).*

H. MORTON & SONS,
Dearne Stores, SCISSETT,
High-Class Grocers and Provision Merchants,
China, Glass, Hardware, Oil and General Dealers.

SPECIAL FOR CHRISTMAS.
ALL FRUIT SPECIALLY CLEANED.

A GOOD SELECTION OF
Toys and Fancy Goods
suitable for Presents.

China, Glass, Crockery, and
Hardware of high-class quality
AT COMPETITIVE PRICES.

A LARGE STOCK OF
Breakfast, Dinner and Tea Services,
Toilet and Trinket Sets.
Fruit Sets
IN NEWEST DESIGNS.

You are respectfully invited to inspect our large and varied Stock.

Morton's Vans bring to your door a large variety of useful Household Goods.

Your Kind Patronage Highly Esteemed.

Local adverts placed by Scissett shops in the early twentieth century. *(L. Robinson collection).*

'Phone: Skelmanthorpe 3137

Agents for

VALOR CONVECTOR HEATERS

J. & A. FIRTH
(Late Horton & Sons)

HIGH CLASS GROCERS &
PROVISION DEALERS

151, Wakefield Road
Scissett

Telephone: Skelmanthorpe 3137

H. MORTON & SONS

* * * *

High Class

Grocers & Provision Dealers

China, Hardware, Oil and
General Merchants

* * * *

SCISSETT

Your local grocers for BETTER SERVICE
High Class GROCERIES and FROSTED FOODS
Dealers in CHINA   ESSO BLUE
and CROCKERY   PARAFFIN
Mobile Shop to all districts.
ALFRED RICHARDSON & SON
Tel.   151, Wakefield Road, Scissett   Skel. 3137

Your "Local" Grocers for BETTER SERVICE
High Class GROCERIES
and FROSTED FOODS
Dealers in CHINA   ESSO BLUE
and CROCKERY   FREE   PARAFFIN
DELIVERIES
G. M. JEFFRIES
Telephone: 151, Wakefield Road, SCISSETT   Skel. 3137

144

The Morton family, circa 1900. Left to right: Stood: Emma Jane Morton, Samuel Morton, ?, ?, ?, ?, ?. Seated: Henrietta Morton(Samuel's wife), Mary Morton(married W Kaye), ?, Henry Morton (founder of shop), ?, ?, ?. Front: Emily Morton, Gladys Morton, Elsie Morton. *(L. Robinson collection).*

Scissett Nortonthorpe chemists shop and also the first post office. *(L. Robinson collection).*

CONDITION POWDERS
FOR HORSES, PIGS, ETC.

Cordial, Physic, Cough, and Staling Ball for Horses, Cleansing Fellon, Stomach and Churning Drinks for Cattle, Foot Rot Mixture, Lambing Oils, Fly, Scab, and Mange Oils for Sheep, Embrocation for Sprains, Bruises, Stiff Joints, etc., in Cattle, etc., Mixture for Scouring in Calves, Roup, etc., Paste, Pills and Powders for Fowls, Distemper, Worm and Condition Powders for Dogs.

PREPARED AND SOLD BY

CHAS. TOWNSEND,
THE DRUG STORES,
SCISSETT and DENBY DALE.

Charles Townsend, Scissett's first chemist. *(L. Robinson collection).*

Local advertisement for Townsend's chemist's. *(L. Robinson collection).*

The chemists shop in later times, at this time run by C Thompson MPS, who was here by 1936. *(L. Robinson collection).*

Ernest Whittle's Milliner's and Draper's shop, around the turn of the nineteenth century. The Crown Hotel is to the left. *(L. Robinson collection).*

A closer view of Ernest Whittle's shop, the front windows are crammed with hats and underwear. *(L. Robinson collection).*

As the window display is identical, this photograph was probably taken on the same day as the latter photograph. The dapper gentleman stood on the kerb outside the shop is Ernest Whittle. *(L. Robinson collection).*

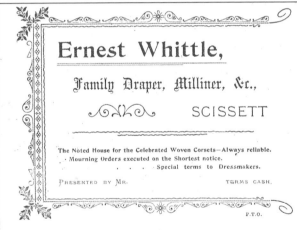

Ernest Whittle,

Family Draper, Milliner, &c.,

SCISSETT

The Noted House for the Celebrated Woven Corsets—Always reliable.

Mourning Orders executed on the Shortest notice.

Special terms to Dressmakers.

PRESENTED BY MR.   TERMS CASH.

P.T.O.

ERNEST WHITTLE
The Draper, Scissett.

INVITES YOU to inspect his large and varied stock of

Millinery, Drapery

and Fancy Goods.

"Always something new," see windows.

Hours of Business—9 a.m. to 8 p.m.

THE FOLLOWING REPRESENT SOME OF THE GOODS STOCKED.

Millinery.	Buckles.	Capes.
Trimmed Hats.	Corsets.	Mantles.
Untrimmed Hats.	Umbrellas.	Mackintoshes.
Sailor Hats.	Furs.	Shawls.
Toques.	Muffs.	Cretonnes.
Children's Bonnets.	Dresses.	Curtains.
Children's Hats.	Blouses.	Sheets.
Flowers.	Dress Skirts.	Counterpanes.
Feathers.	Under Skirts,	Table Cloths.
Ornaments.	Linings.	Table Covers.
Gloves.	Hosiery.	Towellings.
Silk Ties.	Socks.	Turkish Towells.
Lace Ties	Vests.	Huckaback Towells.
Fishues.	Under Clothing.	Pillow Slips.
Collars.	Night Dresses.	Bolster Bases.
Cuffs.	Chemises.	Hardens.
Laces.	Knickers.	Flaxes.
Embroidery.	Combinations.	Linens.
Belts.	Divided Skirts.	Toilet Covers.
Handkerchiefs.	Muslin Aprons.	Side Board Cloths.
Fall Nets.	Cooking Aprons.	Tray Cloths.
Yoke Lace.	Pinafores.	Doyleys.
Chiffon.	Pelisses.	Woollens.
Ribbons.	Coats.	Blankets.
Silks.	Costumes.	Flannels.
Velvets.	Frocks.	Unions.
Trimming.	Tunics.	Flannelette.
Braids,	Jackets.	Shirtings.
Gimps.	Coats.	

Above and left, two local advertisements for Ernest Whittle's shop. *(L. Robinson collection).*

The sign for New Street sits forlornly as the former premises of Ernest Whittle are demolished, circa late 1960's, early 1970's.
(L. Robinson collection).

The Whittle family. Left to right: Back row: Ernest, Joshua (Jos) and May. Front row: Ruth, John, Joseph and Mrs Whittle. In later life, Ernest would regularly be seen walking about Scissett, (after closing the shop, usually at a late hour), walking his companion, a rather fat and elderly spaniel. Ernest was also a staunch supporter of the Clayton West Baptist Chapel where he frequently attended services.
(L. Robinson collection).

After Ernest Whittle's death, the Western part of the premises were occupied by a branch of the Midland Bank. The bank built new premises on the same site whilst retaining the part of the building which they already held. Forty years prior to the bank and before Ernest Whittle's tenure, the western part of the building was occupied by Fred Hirst, a boot and shoemaker and repairer. Mr Hirst installed an old fashioned speaking tube in his shop, through which he communicated to Mrs Hirst, in the kitchen at the back, much to the amusement of the local children.
(L. Robinson collection).

Local advert for Ernest Whittle.
(L. Robinson collection).

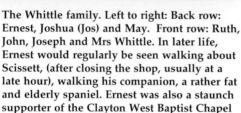

Millinery
New Delivery
All the Latest
Autumn Shades
and Styles

SEE OUR WINDOWS

ERNEST WHITTLE
Scissett

(Prop. - C. S. Armitage.)

WRAY'S XMAS PRESENTS.

Novelties in

Sweets & Boxes of Chocolates

Rowntrees, Terrys and other well-known
Specialities.

GIFT BOOKS,

SCHOOLGIRL'S OWN, RAINBOW,
TIGER TIM,
and all the best Annuals.

CHISTMAS CRACKERS

and lots of attractive lines.

**Beautiful Christmas Cards, Calendars
and Stationery.**

THE NEWSAGENT,

SCISSETT.

WOODWORK OF ALL KINDS

New Work : Repairs : Conversions

We will gladly inspect, advise and
quote, free of charge.

Tel.: Skelmanthorpe 2253   Est. 1906

ISAAC WRAY & SONS

JOINERS : CONTRACTORS
FUNERAL DIRECTORS

Scissett

Near Huddersfield

An archive selection of adverts for local shops and services. *(L. Robinson collection).*

JOINERS, CONTRACTORS
FUNERAL DIRECTORS,
HOUSE FURNISHERS

Tel. Skelmanthorpe 2253

I. Wray & Sons

SCISSETT

Near HUDDERSFIELD

SALES DEPT.

WAKEFIELD ROAD

Wallpapers, Paints, Distempers, Varnish, Brushes of all types, Creosote, Putty, Clear and Horticultural Glass, Plywood, Hardboard.

Roofing Felt from 11/4 roll, Dowelling, Flat Asbestos Sheet, Decorating Sundries.

NEW & SECOND HAND FURNITURE

OPEN UNTIL 6 p.m.   FRIDAY 7 p.m.

An archive selection of adverts for local shops and services. *(L. Robinson collection).*

Edgar and Clara Exley, long time and last proprietors of the fish and chip shop on Stanhope Street. *(L. Robinson collection).*

The Exley's fish and chip shop on Stanhope Street. *(L. Robinson collection).*

Jonas Wilkinson, fish hawker of Scissett. *(L. Robinson collection).*

Jim Hinchliffe, Burhouse's deliveryman, pictured in Kitchenroyd woods. *(L. Robinson collection).*

Mitchell's sweet shop, Barnsley Road. *(L. Robinson collection).*

Willie Brook, by his caravan at Marshall Mill. *(L. Robinson collection).*

Harry Turton, the Scissett post-man, before 1938. *(L. Robinson collection).*

Opening a new drift at Stringer's pit, circa 1890's. *(L. Robinson collection).*

Colliers on their way to Stringer's pit, Wakefield Road. Left to right: Back row; S Dickinson, John W Flack. Front row: George Norton, S Race (who was killed in action in the First World War), J Bridgewater. *(L. Robinson collection).*

William Wood, of Bilham Grange, Clayton West, selling milk in the market place at Scissett. The photograph dates to before 1887 as the milk float stands on land which was used to build four houses in that year. The estimate (supplied by William Hinchliffe) was dated 22 November 1886 quoting a price of £172 for two houses and £335 for four. *(L. Robinson collection).*

William Wood, the son of the William Wood on the latter photograph, still operating the family business, outside Norton's office in 1914. *(L. Robinson collection).*

The third generation of the latter family, the son of the second William Wood. *(L. Robinson collection).*

D C Bunkus, an itinerant quack doctor, selling cough candy, here seen crossing the stile at Langley's.
(L. Robinson collection).

Ernest Flack and his wife, outside the forge at Scissett. *(L. Robinson collection).*

Ernest Flack, the Scissett blacksmith. Ernest was the son of Albert Flack who can be found working as a blacksmith at Scissett in 1912. Ernest was recorded in the trade directory of 1936 in this profession. *(L. Robinson collection).*

The four original partners in the Reliance Motor & Engineering Company outside the original garage on Wakefield Road. Left to right: Willie Shaw, Arthur Hepworth, Harry Bates and Arthur Ackroyd. *(L. Robinson collection).*

The extremely tidy interior of the Reliance garage in 1930. *(L. Robinson collection).*

A 1960's view of the Reliance garage premises. *(L. Robinson collection).*

A later view of the garage premises. *(L. Robinson collection).*

Employees at Joseph Kaye & Sons, rope and twine manufacturers at Wood Street Mills, Scissett in 1904. Left to right: Back row: Mrs Peel, ?, ?, Emma Jane Morton, Mary Morton (later Mrs Kaye). Front row: Tom Peel (boiler firer and engine tenter) with his hands on Gladys Peel. Archie Peel kneels at their side. *(L. Robinson collection)*.

Once the British Queen public house, this building then became the offices of Edward Blackburn Ltd, dyers and twisters. The photograph depicts later re-use by Beaumont Blending Co. Ltd., loose stock dyers. *(L. Robinson collection)*.

The Norton brothers, Top o' th' Hill Mill, handloom-weaving shed. It was later re-used by Edward Blackburn Ltd (cotton doublers) as a winding, reeling and twisting mill. *(L. Robinson collection).*

Edward Blackburn Ltd, Top o' th' Hill Mill, employees circa 1920. Fifth from the left on the back row is Annie Bedford. Sat on the far right of the front row is Annie Hardcastle, who can be seen in the following photograph, nearly 50 years later. *(L. Robinson collection).*

The last day at Edward Blackburn Ltd, Top o' th' Hill Mill, September 1966. Left to right: Herbert Tinker, Nora Marsden, Ethel Firth, Margaret Firth, Marjorie Barraclough, Thelma Conway, Vivian Walsh, Gracie Firth, Annie Hardcastle, Walter Hardcastle. *(L. Robinson collection).*

The last day at Edward Blackburn Ltd, dye house, Ings Mill, Union Street, September 1966. The employees are Herbert Jones, George Coates, Lewis Dearnley and Eric Lee.

(L. Robinson collection).

The Vicar of Scissett, Rev. W P Kingston, was a keen cricketer during his tenure of St. Augustine's between 1903–1907. *(L. Robinson collection).*

Joe Rushforth, a member of Rev. Kingston's team. *(L. Robinson collection).*

Harry Webb, a member of Rev. Kingston's team. *(L. Robinson collection).*

David Jones, a member of Rev. Kingston's team and also the landlord of the British Queen. *(L. Robinson collection).*

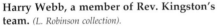

Scissett Cricket team, taken between 1914 and 1922. Left to right: Back row: Bertie Shaw, Harold White, Arthur Flack, Charlie Blackburn, Henry Horton, Arthur Battye, Rev. J V Haswell (Parson 1914–1922). Front row: Clarence Blackburn, Wilfred Flack, G W Hirst, Bob Blackburn, Friend Wilkinson. *(L. Robinson collection)*.

Nortonthorpe Cricket Club 1929/30. Left to right: Back row: Jonas Woodhead, Robert (Bob) Blackburn, Friend Garratt, John Redgewick, Robert (Robbie) Doyle, Jack Wray, George Clay, Willie Firth, Josiah (Jos) Whittle, Willie Shaw. Front row: Dennis Blackburn, George Woodhouse (or Woodhead), Geoffrey Blackburn, William (Willie) Archer, Cecil Taylor, Charles (Charlie) Blackburn, Rowland Hill, Arthur Battye, Cecil Shaw. *(L. Robinson collection)*.

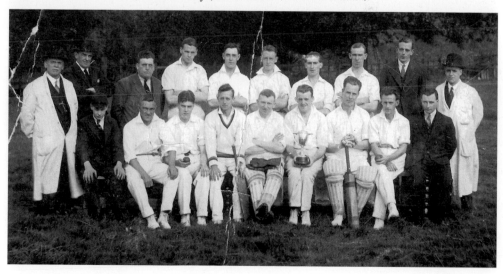

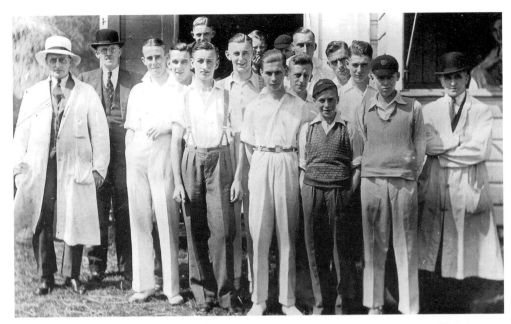

Nortonthorpe Cricket team, circa 1934. Left to right: In the doorway at the back: Ralph Johnson, George Dawson, Spencer Armitage. Left to right: Mr Dyson (umpire), Arthur Dawson, Albert Wood, Harold Schofield, Ronnie Bentley, Jeffrey Whittel, Dennis Blackburn, Willie Archer, Harold Blackburn, ?, Richard Littlewood, Donald White, ?? Kenworthy (umpire).
(L. Robinson collection).

Nortonthorpe Rugby Football team 1891 at the Queen's Head Inn. Left to right: In the doorway: Mr Needham, Isaac Wragg. Back row: A Peace, C Littlewood, Joe Rushforth, ?, A Senior, ?, A Burhouse, J Shaw. Middle row: T Pell, H Hirst, W Morley, T Morley, A Morris, N Morris. Front row: J W Bedford, D Jones. *(L. Robinson collection).*

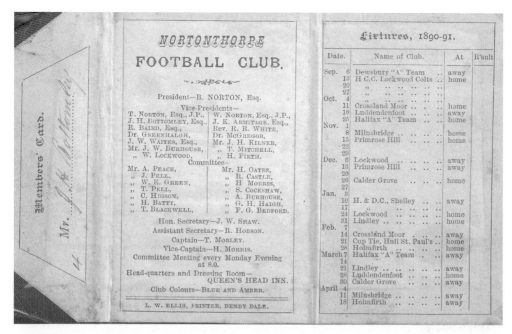

NORTONTHORPE

FOOTBALL CLUB.

President—B. NORTON, Esq.

Vice-Presidents—
T. NORTON, Esq., J.P., | W. NORTON, Esq., J.P.,
J. H. BOTTOMLEY, Esq., | J. K. ARMITAGE, Esq.,
R. BAIRD, Esq., | Rev. R. R. WHITE,
Dr. GREENHALGH, | Dr. McGREGOR,
J. W. WAITES, Esq., | Mr. J. H. KILNER,
Mr. J. W. BURHOUSE, | „ T. MITCHELL,
„ W. LOCKWOOD, | „ H. FIRTH.

Committee—
Mr. A. PEACE, | Mr. H. OATES,
„ J. PELL, | „ R. CASTLE,
„ W. E. GREEN, | „ H MORRIS,
„ T. PELL, | „ S. COCKSHAW,
„ C. HIGSON, | „ A. BURHOUSE,
„ H. BATTY, | „ G. H. HAIGH,
„ T. BLACKWELL, | „ F. G. BEDFORD.

Hon. Secretary—J. W. SHAW.
Assistant Secretary—R. HOBSON.
Captain—T. MORLEY.
Vice-Captain—H. MORRIS.
Committee Meeting every Monday Evening at 8.0.
Head-quarters and Dressing Room—
QUEEN'S HEAD INN.

Club Colours—BLUE AND AMBER.

L. W. ELLIS, PRINTER, DENBY DALE.

Fixtures, 1890-91.

Date.	Name of Club.	At	R'sult
Sep. 6	Dewsbury "A" Team	away	
13	H C.C. Lockwood Colts	home	
20	„ „ „		
27	„ „ „		
Oct. 4	„ „ „		
11	Crossland Moor	home	
18	Luddendenfoot	away	
25	Halifax "A" Team	home	
Nov. 1	„ „ „		
8	Milnsbridge	home	
15	Primrose Hill	home	
22			
29			
Dec. 6	Lockwood	away	
13	Primrose Hill	away	
20			
26	Calder Grove	home	
27			
Jan. 3			
10	H. & D.C., Shelley	away	
17	„ „ „		
24	Lockwood	home	
31	Lindley	home	
Feb. 7			
14	Crossland Moor	away	
21	Cup Tie, Hull St. Paul's	home	
28	Holmfirth	home	
March 7	Halifax "A" Team	away	
14			
21	Lindley	away	
28	Luddendenfoot	home	
30	Calder Grove	away	
April 4			
11	Milnsbridge	away	
18	Holmfirth	away	

(left margin) Members' Card. Mr. .... J. H. Bottomley

Nortonthorpe Football Club fixture card for the 1890/91 season. This card once belonged to J H Bottomley, a director of Norton Bros. & Co. between 1875 and 1895. *(L. Robinson collection).*

Nortonthorpe Cricket and Football Club, Officials and Fixture list 1891/2. *(L. Robinson collection).*

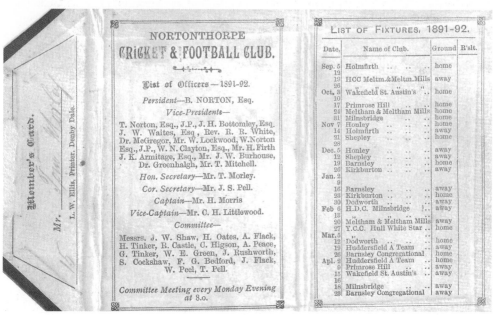

NORTONTHORPE

CRICKET & FOOTBALL CLUB.

List of Officers — 1891-92.

President—B. NORTON, Esq.

Vice-Presidents—
T. Norton, Esq., J.P., J. H. Bottomley, Esq.
J. W. Waites, Esq, Rev. R. R. White,
Dr. McGregor, Mr. W. Lockwood, W. Norton
Esq., J.P., W. N. Clayton, Esq., Mr. H. Firth
J. K. Armitage, Esq., Mr. J. W. Burhouse,
Dr. Greenhalgh, Mr. T. Mitchell.

Hon. Secretary—Mr. T. Morley.
Cor. Secretary—Mr. J. S. Pell.
Captain—Mr. H. Morris
Vice-Captain—Mr. C. H. Littlewood.

Committee—
Messrs. J. W. Shaw, H. Oates, A. Flack,
H. Tinker, R. Castle, C. Higson, A. Peace,
G. Tinker, W. E. Green, J. Rushworth,
S. Cockshaw, F. G. Bedford, J. Flack,
W. Peel, T. Pell.

Committee Meeting every Monday Evening at 8.o.

LIST OF FIXTURES, 1891-92.

Date.	Name of Club.	Ground	R'slt.
Sep. 5	Holmfirth	home	
12			
19	HCC Meltm.&Meltm. Mills	away	
26			
Oct. 3	Wakefield St. Austin's	home	
10			
17	Primrose Hill	home	
24	Meltham & Meltham Mills	home	
31	Milnsbridge	home	
Nov. 7	Honley	home	
14	Holmfirth	away	
21	Shepley	home	
28			
Dec. 5	Honley	away	
12	Shepley	away	
19	Barnsley	home	
26	Kirkburton	away	
Jan. 2			
9			
16	Barnsley	away	
23	Kirkburton	home	
30	Dodworth	away	
Feb. 6	H.D.C. Milnsbridge	away	
13			
20	Meltham & Meltham Mills	away	
27	Y.C.C. Hull White Star	home	
Mar. 5			
12	Dodworth	away	
19	Huddersfield A Team	away	
26	Barnsley Congregational	home	
Apl. 2	Huddersfield A Team	home	
9	Primrose Hill	away	
15	Wakefield St. Austin's	away	
16			
18	Milnsbridge	away	
23	Barnsley Congregational	away	

(left margin) Member's Card. L. W. Ellis, Printer, Denby Dale. Mr. ....

Nortonthorpe Rugby Football Club 1893/4. The photograph was taken to commemorate the team winning the Holliday Charities Cup in season 1893/4. Left to right: Back row: W Turner, W Morley, G Dickinson, W Hirst, T Pell, A Senior, A Morris, J W Bedford, A Peace. Seated: C Littlewood, T Morley, G H Green, C Peace, J Rushforth, G F Perkins, J H Craven. Front row: D Jones, A Dyson. *(L. Robinson collection).*

Scissett AFC circa 1900/1902. Their playing field was behind the Crown Inn, the photograph was also taken behind the Crown. Left to right: Back row: Ike Wareham, Arthur Dawson, Bertie Barraclough, Johnny Jones. Middle row: ?, N Barraclough, Clarence Blackburn, Percy Firth, ?. Front row: ?, Joe Rushforth, ?. *(L. Robinson collection).*

Nortonthorpe AFC 1902, their playing field was behind the church. Left to right; Back row: F Schofield, P Barraclough, J Jones, D Jones, F Dawson, T L Jones, W H Whittel, B Barraclough, Rev. W P Kingston. Front row: G Bridgewater (linesman), E Barraclough, H Barker, C Boulton, Ed. Blackburn, George Robinson. Nortonthorpe Football club, later to become Scissett AFC was formed largely due to the efforts of the Rev. W P Kingston and Mr A F Jay (schoolmaster). During their first season the team played only friendly games. They then joined the Huddersfield and District League in Division 2. They didn't win a game during that first season but later gained promotion to Division 1 and won the Championship Shield in 1911, 1912 and 1913. Their first secretary was Mr B Barraclough. *(L. Robinson collection).*

Scissett AFC taken on the vicarage lawn in 1907. The playing field was behind the church. Left to right: Back row: ?, Clarence Blackburn, P Barker, ?, ?, Arthur Priest, ?, Joe Wray. Front row: ?? Barraclough, P Firth, Ernest Battye, Stan Hudson. *(L. Robinson collection).*

Scissett AFC – Winners of the Huddersfield and District League 1910/11. Taken on the vicarage lawn, left to right: Back row: V Dickenson, G H Dawson, Joe Wray. Middle row: W Flack, P Exley, B Barraclough, P Barker, W Lockwood, F Wilkinson, ?, J W Peel, F Priest, A Hinchliffe, A Wharam. Front row: E Battye, C Blackburn, M Barker, P Barraclough, Stan Hudson, A Priest, F Ellis, J Firth. Left to right of the shield are P Firth and S Race. *(L. Robinson collection).*

Scissett AFC taken on the Vicarage lawn, team and officials. Winners of Huddersfield and District League 1911/12. Left to right; Back row: E Battye, G H Dawson, F Dawson, ?, ?, W Flack. Middle row: ?, ?, ?, ?, J Firth, ?, ?. Front row: M Barker, H Firth, F Wilkinson, ?, ?, B Barraclough, H Barker. With the shield, left to right are D Firth and S Hudson. *(L. Robinson collection).*

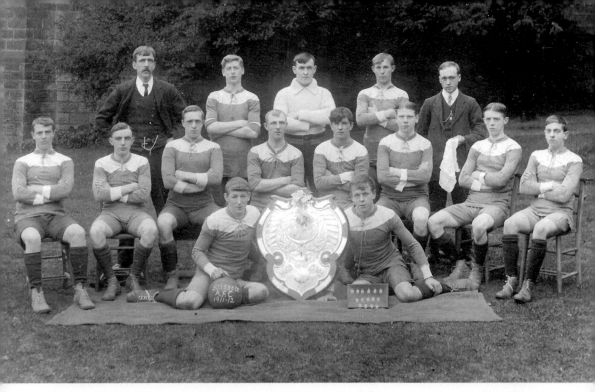

Scissett AFC, as above but without team officials. *(L. Robinson collection).*

Scissett AFC taken in front of the Queen's Head Inn. Winners of the Huddersfield & District League 1912/13. Left to right: Back row: F Buckley, P Hirst, F Wilkinson. Middle row: W Dickenson, G N Dawson, F Dawson, H Firth, M Barker, J Firth, W Crossland (the landlord of the Queen's – holding baby Tom Crossland), Tom Burhouse. Front row: D Jackson (killed during World War One), D Firth, S Jackson, S Hudson, H Barker. *(L. Robinson collection).*

Scissett AFC in front of the Crown Hotel, circa 1932. Left to right: Back row: A Mitchell, H Hollingworth, F Morley, D Robinson, H Dearnley, B Doyle, G Barraclough, A Blakey, T Rusby (landlord of the Crown), E Whittles, N Beaumont, J Woodhead, P Rawlings, T Hellewell, L Cook, A Sykes, F Tinker, F Craven, F Garratt, ?. Front row: C Webb, W Beaumont, H Wray, W Tinker, R Hill, B Morley, R Machin, C Clay, J Hudson, W Hollingworth, ?. L Dearnley is seated holding the trophy. *(L. Robinson collection).*

Kitchenroyd Amateurs AFC Members Card. *(L. Robinson collection).*

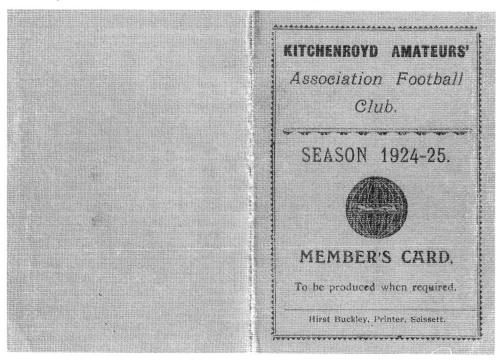

KITCHENROYD AMATEURS'

Association Football Club.

SEASON 1924-25.

MEMBER'S CARD.

To be produced when required.

Hirst Buckley, Printer, Scissett.

List of Officials.

President:

G. H. NORTON, Esq,

Vice-Presidents:

G. Hellewell, Esq., Dr. Bleasdell, Dr. Archibald,
G. T. Hellewell, Esq., P. R. Jackson, Esq., W. H.
Whittell, Esq., T. Norton, Esq., W. Fisher, Esq.,
R. Walshaw, Esq., C. Harnwell, Esq., W. H.
Kaye, Esq,, Capt. T. St. J. Belbin,

Hon. Secretary : G, Woodhouse.

Hon. Treasurer : B. Hollingworth

Committee :

Messrs. F. Fisher, R. Hill, G. W, Hirst, F.
Garratt, A. Hodgson, Jas. Taylor, W. Dyson, R.
Armitage, W. Hollingworth.

M ......4. 9............................

DATE	NAME OF CLUB.	AT	F	A
LIST OF FIXTURES.				
SECOND TEAM.				
1924.				
Sep. 20	Scissett ......7-1.......	home		
27	Clayton West..	home		
Oct. 4	Fenay Bridge....0...........	away		
11	Shepley...........6-0......	home		
18	Skelmanthorpe A.......	away		
25	Kirkburton Y.M.B.C......	home		
Nov. 1	Emley Moor	home		
8	Flockton Juniors	away		
15	1st Round Hudds. Cup ...			
22				
29	Scissett ....2-3......	away		
Dec. 6	Clayton West........	away		
13				
20	Fenay Bridge ..2-1...	home		
27	Shepley......	away		
1925.				
Jan. 3	Skelmanthorpe A....4-1...	home		
10	Kirkburton Y.M.B.C	away		
17	Emley Moor	away		
24	1st Round D.V. Cup			
31	Flockton Juniors ...0-....	home		
Feb. 7				
14				
21				
28				
Mar. 7				
14				
21				

Kitchenroyd Amateurs AFC Officials and Fixtures 1924/5. *(L. Robinson collection).*

**Scissett AFC 1934/5 in front of the Crown Inn. Left to right: Back row: H Harrop, G Smith,
J Woodhead, E Newton, E Whittles, W Beaumont, H Hollingworth, A Blakey, G Barraclough,
T Rusby, A Beever, F Tinker, L Cook, A Gunson, P Rawlings, D Robinson. Front row: W Addy,
J Hudson, H Bowden, G Moorehouse, H Dearnley, J Metcalfe, R Machin, C Clay, F Craven,
W Hollingworth.** *(L. Robinson collection).*

Scissett AFC in the long room at the Crown Inn in 1967/8. *(L. Robinson collection).*

Scissett AFC – 1935 Barnsley Challenge Cup. The team are pictured before the match which was played at 'Oakwell', home of Barnsley AFC. Left to right: Back row: H Dearnley, A Beever, J Woodhead, A Blakey, L Cook. Front row: W Beaumont, H Bowden, G Moorehouse, J W Metcalfe, R Machin, C Clay. (Scissett lost to Highstone Rovers 4-1) *(L. Robinson collection).*

Scissett Amateur Operatic Society – 'Don Quixote' 1930. Left to right: Back row: B Dickinson, A Wood, G Wray, A Dransfield, H Wray, H Brook, S Wray, A Dawson, G Barraclough, R Grayson, W Dickinson, ?. Main group: B Littlewood, A Battye, A Hardcastle, V Dransfield, Mrs Tyas, ?, Mrs Firth, M Littlewood, L Jones, ?, A Eastwood, G Wood, J Senior, B Bentley, J Woodhead, ?, ?, C Bell, E Greaves, Mrs Senior, C Battye, W Shaw, D Battye, K Robinson, Mr Woodhall, A Mellor, H Mitchell, ?, ?. Front row: G H Dawson, Miss Taylor, C Blackburn, ?, ?, L Birkinshaw, donkey!, G Wray, A Green, W Senior, V Smith, E Shaw. *(L. Robinson collection).*

Scissett Amateur Operatic Society. Left to right: C Blackburn, donkey!, ?, ?, ?, ?, A Mellor, J Woodhead, C Bell, C Battye, G Wood, M Littlewood, B Bentley, A Eastwood, ?, ?, Mrs Firth, ?, ?, ?, ?, ?, ?, L Birkinshaw. *(L. Robinson collection).*

Scissett Amateur Operatic Society circa 1930's. Left to right: Alice Blackburn, Spencer Armitage, ?, Rowland Hill, ?, Frank Armitage, Mary Littlewood, Hubert Barraclough, Marjorie Wood, Albert Wood, Jannie Woodhead, Reggie Grayson. *(L. Robinson collection).*

Scissett Amateur Operatic Society – 'Floradora' 1932. Left to right: Stephen Wray, Hubert Barraclough, Albert Dransfield, Vincent Firth, Alec Wood. *(L. Robinson collection).*

Scissett Amateur Operatic Society – 'Floradora' 1932. Officials and Principals, left to right: Back row: Beaumont Littlewood (stage manager), Willie Shaw (electrician), Stephen Wray, Vincent Firth, Albert Dransfield, Hubert Barraclough, Alec Wood, Arthur Hardcastle (props), Henry Mitchell (pianist). Front row: Vivian Smith (school teacher, organiser and producer), Annie Battye, Mrs M Tyas, Willie Senior (conductor & musical director), Grace Wray, Evelyn Dransfield, Mrs E Taylor (wardrobes). *(L. Robinson collection).*

Scissett Amateur Operatic Society – 'Floradora' 1932. Vincent Firth and Mrs M Tyas on stage. *(L. Robinson collection).*

Scissett Amateur Operatic Society – an unknown performance, circa 1930's. *(L. Robinson collection).*

Scissett Amateur Operatic Society – 'Floradora' 1932. Left to right: Back row: A Dawson, F Armitage, R Hill, S Armitage, G Barraclough, H Barraclough, R Grayson, A Wood, G Wray. Front row: V Dransfield, Mrs Firth, R Shaw, A Eastwood, ?, ?, ?, ?, D Battye, ? *(L. Robinson collection).*

Scissett Amateur Operatic Society – 'Wildflower' 1936. Left to right: ?, Marjorie Wood, ?, Grace Wray, Reggie Grayson, Lambert's donkey, Stephen Wray, Jannie Woodhead, Hubert Barraclough, E Dransfield, Vincent Firth. *(L. Robinson collection).*

Scissett Amateur Operatic Society – 'No No Nanette' 1938. Left to right: Back row: J Bower, D Flack, D Newton, ?, A Wood, M Taylor, R Grayson, E Shaw, R Sainter, G H Dawson. Front row: E Turton, D Beaumont, R Bell, M Wood, K Wainwright, A Dransfield, E Dickenson, M Rhodes, P Wray, G Pell, L Pearson. *(L. Robinson collection).*

Scissett Amateur Operatic Society – 'Victoria and her Hussar' 1939. Left to right: Marjorie Taylor, Stephen Wray, Albert Dransfield, Hubert Barraclough, Grace Wray, Evelyn Dransfield, Vincent Firth. *(L. Robinson collection).*

Scissett Amateur Operatic Society circa mid 1960's present 'Good Night Vienna'. Left to right: Back row: Lindsey Guy, S Thomas, M Hampsall, P Wadsworth, P Turner, Brian Johnson, M Newsome, A Stone, Jill Copley, T Mclaughlin, R Littlewood, M Wray, B Roe, K Turner, J Shotton, M Griffiths, C Shaw, Nicholas Adamski. Front row: T Johnson, R Senior, J Johnson, L Ramsden, C Noble, M Tann, L Morley, K Harvey, ?, ?, ?, ?. *(L. Robinson collection).*

Nortonthorpe Athletic Festival 1909, the runner nearest the camera is Norman Lodge.
(L. Robinson collection).

Above and below, Nortonthorpe Athletic Festival 1909. *(L. Robinson collection).*

Nortonthorpe Athletic Festival 1909. The man sat with his legs stretched out on the grass is Herbert Firth. *(L. Robinson collection).*

Nortonthorpe Athletic Festival 1909. *(L. Robinson collection).*

NORTONTHORPE
Flower Show & Athletic Sports

SATURDAY, AUGUST 12th, 1911.

Local Attractions :--

Coronation and
Empire Pageant

performed by about 100 well trained Local
Children, at 2-15. **Tableaux, Mazing,
Musical, Rifle,** and **Physical Drills,**
etc.

Amateur - - -
Footballers' Race

for Members of Clubs within a three miles
radius. To be run in **full Football
Costume,** for **Medals value** about
£2 10s. 0d.

— ALSO —

Schoolboys' Race

for **Watches value** £1 10s. 0d.

BERT BARRACLOUGH, Sec.

I. WRAY, PRINTER, SCISSETT.

NORTONTHORPE
AND DISTRICT
AGRICULTURAL & FLORAL SOCIETY'S
Athletic Festival

UNDER A.A.A LAWS AND N.C.U. RULES,
HELD IN THE

CRICKET FIELD,
SCISSETT, Near HUDDERSFIELD,
ON
Saturday, Aug. 13th, 1927,
Commencing at 3 p.m.

N. T. Beardsell, Esq., & Miss Senior,

assisted by Rev. H. C. Libbey,

have kindly consented to distributed the Prizes
after the final of each event.

*A Special train leaves Huddersfield to
Clayton West 1-45. Returning 7-40.*

Programme - 2d.

**Programme cover for Nortonthorpe Flower
and Athletic Shows, 1911.** *(L. Robinson collection).*

**The programme cover for the 1927 (and final)
Nortonthorpe Athletic Festival.** *(L. Robinson collection).*

**The Scissett (H)'It' girls of 1930. Left to
right: Mary Crossland, Mildred Blackburn,
Ruth Whittle, Marjorie Taylor, Annie
Battye, Phyllis Wood, Gladys Wood.**
(L. Robinson collection).

Wilford Kaye's gymnasium club, performing at Scissett Flower Show, circa 1905. The club's headquarters was at Wood Street Mills. Numbered 1 is Wilford Kaye, 2 is H Barker and 3 is F Wilkinson. *(L. Robinson collection).*

Scissett Working Men's Club billiards team, circa 1935. Left to right: Back row: Charles Lewis Bentley, Herbert Wood, Horace Wray, George Woodhouse, Arthur Tinker. Front row: Wilfred Addy, Sydney Robinson, Geoffrey Blackburn, Arthur Dearnley, Jack Hudson, Jack Battye. *(L. Robinson collection).*

The muffin seller at Scissett Flower Show in 1910. *(L. Robinson collection).*

Scene from the Empire Pageant, Scissett, 1911. *(L. Robinson collection).*

Above and below scenes from the Empire Pageant, Scissett, 1911. *(L. Robinson collection).*

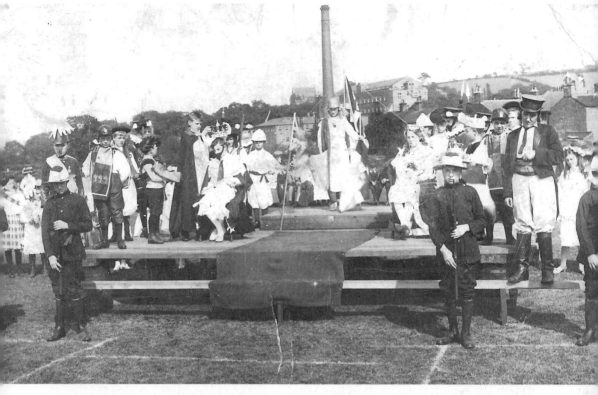

Scene from the Empire Pageant, Scissett, 1911. *(L. Robinson collection).*

Volunteer nurses at the Denby Dale soldiers convalescent home during the First World War. Back row: ?, ?, ?, A Wray, ?, P Wray. Front row: unknown. *(L. Robinson collection).*

The Penistone volunteers await their train at Penistone station, in order to join up with the army during the First World War. The volunteers included a number of men from Scissett. *(L. Robinson collection).*

First World War peace celebrations at Scissett, passing the Co-Op in 1919. The village had lost a number of sons. Those who did not return are listed in the notes on Scissett at the end of this book. *(L. Robinson collection).*

Nortonthorpe Mills from the air. Highbridge comes in from the left and crosses over to Cuttlehurst on the right. The photograph was taken for the Illustrated Review, London in 1939. *(L. Robinson collection).*

Male employees gather at Nortonthorpe, all of whom were veterans of the First World War, ready for the visit of Lord Lascelles during the 1920's. *(S. Sheead collection).*

Scissett, from Cuttlehurst Mill, circa 1920. The nearest chimney belonged to the gas-house. The middle chimney was that of Kaye's band and twine works. The far chimney belonged to Ed. Blackburn's dye works. Fleet Street can be seen in the background. The derrick, used for carrying coal by air from Nortonthorpe colliery to Norton's mill can be seen in the right foreground. *(L. Robinson collection).*

View from Rock Villas, Scissett, 1930. Nortonthorpe Low Cross sheds are to the left. In the centre are Kaye's, Wood Street Mills – twine and rope works. To the right is Ed. Blackburn's, Ings Mill, dye works. *(L. Robinson collection).*

Norton's Bottom Low Cross being demolished, circa 1950. *(L. Robinson collection).*

Supplementary Chronology

Denby Dale

1869 – 3 April – Appointment of Overseers and Constables for Staincross Division

Overseers:
Clayton West – D Schofield & John Lee, Cumberworth – W Box & D Peace, Denby – J Haigh
& E Smithson, Gunthwaite – J Milnes & B Fish, Ingbirchworth – T Taylor & C Webster.

Constables:
Clayton West – D Schofield & R Moxon, Cumberworth – Thomas Senior & David Marsden,
Denby – Jos. Haigh & Henry Haigh, Gunthwaite – B Fish, Ingbirchworth – Wm. Holmes.

1869 – 22 May – The Denby Dale Viaduct
At the monthly meeting of the Huddersfield Town Council, which was held on Monday
last, the question of the unsafe state of the Denby Dale viaduct was discussed. The subject
was moved by Ald. Brooke, who moved 'that the Town Clerk address a communication to
the Lancashire and Yorkshire Railway Company on the part of this council, calling their
attention to the insecure and unsatisfactory state of the Denby Dale viaduct, on their
Huddersfield and Penistone line, which is the main route of passenger communication
between this borough and London; that the Company be called upon to take immediate
measures for the reconstruction of the viaduct in stone; and that, failing an assurance from
them to that effect, a report be addressed to the Board of Trade, and such other proceedings
taken as shall be requisite to the effect of the above object. Ald. Day seconded the motion
and it was carried unanimously. The undertaking will be of rather an expensive character,
as the viaduct crosses the valley at a high altitude in Denby Dale, and extends for a
considerable space.

1869 – 19 June – Liberal Demonstration at Denby Dale
On Saturday the Liberal electors of Denby Dale celebrated, by a tea party, the return of Lord
Milton and Mr Beaumont, members for the South West Riding and the defeat of the
petitions at Wakefield. The meeting was held in the weaving shed belonging to Messrs.
Brownhill and Scatchard, who had kindly lent it for the purposes of the demonstration.

1869 – 6 November – Alleged Game Trespass at Denby Dale
John Burdett, cartwright, of Denby Dale and Geo. Thomas Peace, of the same place, were
charged with a game trespass on Tuesday the 19th ult. The information was laid by
Jonathan Norton, watcher for Mr Marchant of Huddersfield, who has some shooting in that
district. Jonathan Norton stated that Mr Marchant had the shooting over some land
belonging to Mr Bosville at Denby. On the 19th ult. he saw the defendants inside Hag
Wood. Witness was about 100 yards from them. He heard them discharge a gun. They then
shifted and went into a by-lane, from which they proceeded to some other fields also
belonging to Mr Bosville. The one was a pasture and the other a mowing field. Burdett had
a gun and Peace had a stick with which he was beating the hedges. He caught them as they

came out of the field and charged them with trespassing. When he did so, Burdett threatened to blow his brains out if he said anything. Peace said nothing. They fired at some pigeons afterwards. There were partridges preserved in that field. Witness was by himself on that occasion. Witness stated that he was a quarryman. He was charged with poaching in 1866 but the case was dismissed. He was three months in York castle in 1852 for an assault. This was the case for the prosecution. Mr Barrett said his clients positively denied trespassing in search of game at all. Peace did not himself keep a gun, but he told one of his father's servants to go up into the pigeon cot and catch some pigeons for him. He caught one, and he and Burdett went out to the lane with it. Burdett had a gun. So far was it from their intention to trespass that when they got out they found they had no caps with them and they went and borrowed one. Peace fired at the pigeon while they were in the lane, and afterwards crossed into the field in search of it. Herbert Wild, who works for Mr Peace, senior, stated that on Tuesday the 19th ult. that he went into the pigeon cot at the request of Mr Peace, junior (the defendant) and caught one pigeon for him to shoot at. He saw the defendants go up the lane. Peace had the gun, but no dogs. Witness gave the pigeon to Burdett who carried it until they got a little way up the lane, and then threw it up. Peace shot the pigeon. John Crossland, weaver, said he kept pigeons. He knew the watcher, Norton. On Saturday, the 23rd ult. he saw Norton, who told him that he had seen Peace and Burdett shooting pigeons, and he meant to have them up for it. He said nothing about game. George Wood, who had been in company with Crossland, gave corroborative evidence. The defendants were discharged on paying the costs, 22s.

(George Thomas was the son of James Peace, manufacturer at Inkerman Mill)

1870 – 2 April – Appointment of Overseers of the Poor and Constables

Overseers:
Clayton West – James Wickson and David Schoefield, Cumberworth – William Box and David Peace, Denby – Joseph Haigh and Erasmus Smithson, Gunthwaite – Thomas Mills and John Mills (Milnes?), High Hoyland – W H Morrison and Thomas Holden, Ingbirchworth – Thomas Crookes and Charles Webster.

Constables:
Clayton West – David Schoefield and John Hargrave, Cumberworth – Thomas Senior and David Marsden, Denby – Henry Haigh, Gunthwaite – Thomas Mills (Milnes?), High Hoyland – Richard Fountain, Ingbirchworth – William Holmes.

1870 – 2 April – Forester's funeral at Denby Dale

The interment of Mr Frederick Brierley, dyer, Denby Dale, a member of the Ancient Order of Foresters and also of the Oddfellow's Society, took place on Sunday last, at Cumberworth church in the family vault. The funeral cortege began to move from Denby Dale a few minutes before twelve at noon for Cumberworth church, a distance of nearly two miles preceded by the members of the Court Undaunted, No. 819 of Clayton West; the members from the Courts at Cumberworth, Shelley, Shepley and Honley; and likewise the members of the Independent Order of Oddfellows at Denby Dale. The procession, which was computed to comprise 500 persons of all ranks, was officially conducted by Mr Joseph Whitaker, surveyor, of Denby Dale; Mr John Kenworthy, churchwarden of Shelley, and Mr Wm. Peace, manufacturer of of Shepley. The church at Cumberworth was crowded in every part, and the solemn burial service was conducted the Rev. Wm. Hirst, in a very impressive manner. The late Mr Frederick Brierley was 35 years of age, and he has left a widow and three children to mourn his loss.

1870 – 16 April – A Glorious Conservative victory at Denby

This township (Denby) has been the scene of much excitement during the past week in consequence of a severe conflict for the office of poor law guardians. The election has assumed a political complexion in consequence of the efforts of the Liberal party to displace Mr H C Dickinson, Chairman of the Scissett Conservative Association, and to elect in his place, Mr Z Hinchliffe, the local Radical leader. Not withstanding the loud boasts of the Liberals, and several weeks of hard canvassing, the poll shows the great preponderance of Conservative feeling in this township. H Dickinson (Conservative) 155, J Kilner (Conservative) 144, Jas. Peace (Conservative) 96, Z Hinchliffe (Liberal) 88. The first two were elected.

1870 – 21 May – A Denby Dale Case – Tale of a Pig

The plaintiff was Thomas Lockwood, a weaver residing at Denby Dale, the defendant Charles Roodhouse, a mason living at Nortonthorpe. Mr Tyas appeared for the plaintiff. It appeared that on the 29th January last, the plaintiff sold the defendant a pig which at the time he warranted to be sound, and although his attention was called to the pig being lame, he said it had been strained. The pig was to be delivered in a fortnight but the weather being very rough the plaintiff kept it for three weeks. At the end of that time it was delivered and in three weeks afterwards it died from diseased lungs. The defendant on being called denied that he warranted the pig. The defendant called Hugh Wilby who made a *post mortem!* examination, and Mr Smith, veterinary surgeon, residing at Darton both of whom said the pig must have been ailing for several months and the disease must have been known to the defendant. Verdict for plaintiff with costs of witnesses.

1870 – 23 July – Serious Colliery Explosion near Barnsley

Yesterday (Friday) a serious explosion of gas took place at a day pit, the property of Mr Stanhope at Low Mill, Cawthorne. It appears that the working has been suspended some few months and yesterday, three gentlemen, Messrs. Enoch Taylor, Henry Ellis and George Wood, went to examine the pit, probably with a view of working the same. They proceeded down the day hole, having a naked candle, when suddenly an explosion of gas occurred, by which all were seriously hurt. Aid was secured, and every means to alleviate their suffering was exerted, but, owing to the serious nature of the injuries, some time must elapse before the sufferers can recover. Up to the time of writing we are informed that Mr Taylor is in a precarious state.

1870 – 6 August – The Serious Colliery Explosion near Barnsley – Death of Mr Ellis

The serious explosion in the Sovereign colliery at Cawthorne on Saturday week, has terminated fatally in the case of Mr Henry Ellis, colliery proprietor of Denby Dale. It will be remembered that the deceased and two other gentlemen went into the workings of the pit with a candle, when an explosion took place, burning all of them. The deceased was taken to his home, and since the accident has been attended to by Drs. Rowley and Firth; but so serious were his injuries that he died on Sunday evening. He was 60 years of age and greatly respected. The inquest was held at Denby Dale on Tuesday before Thomas Taylor, Esq. Coroner, when a verdict of accidental death was returned. From the evidence it appears that the deceased went into the workings with a naked candle after he had been warned not to do so. Mr Enoch Taylor, another of the sufferers, still lies at Denby in a precarious state; but Mr Wood of Shipley, the third party injured, is reported to be improving.

Since the above was in type we regret to learn that Mr Taylor has also succumbed to the injuries received, his death taking place on Thursday.

1870 – 15 October – Breach of License at Denby Dale

David Green, Railway Inn, beer-house, Denby Dale, was charged with having his house open for the sale of drink at half past eleven on the night of the 24th ult. Mr Freeman defended. PC Worsley stated that at half past eleven on the evening of the above day he was on duty near the Railway Inn, Denby Dale, kept by the defendant, when he saw a woman named Hannah Beevers go up to the front door and knock at it. The door was opened by the defendant and the woman asked for a pint of beer, at the same time handing him a can. He got the beer and had given it into her hands but as soon as he (the officer) made his appearance he took it from her, and returning with it to the house placed it under a seat. Witness entered the house and found two men sitting drinking. He asked the landlord how he accounted for them being there, and he replied that they were travellers just arrived from Bradford and intended remaining all night. He watched the house outside and at twelve saw these men come out and go into the White Hart, having had an invitation to do so from the landlord's son. This was the case for the prosecution.

Hannah Beevers, the woman referred to by last witness denied that the defendant supplied her with any beer. She had gone to an adjoining shop to purchase some goods before eleven o'clock but stopped too long and when she got to defendant's house he would not let her have it. The consequence was that she left the can with him, intending to return for it next morning. Thomas Beevers, one of the men who had been in the house was called to prove that he and his companion were bone fide travellers, but Supt. Sykes said he would go upon the case as concerned the woman only, assuming that the men were travellers. He found that the defendant had been summoned on a similar charge in 1866. Defendant said that was only a friendly case to test the point as to whether he could keep his house open until eleven o'clock at night. Fined 10s and costs.

The Peace manufacturing family of Denby Dale

James Peace married Narah Horton on 26th November 1830 at Penistone.

In White's 1857 and 1866 directories James and Joseph Peace (who were first cousins) are noted to woollen manufacturers in Denby Dale. On 14th January 1867, Joseph died suddenly, though his wife, Mary was noted in the Post Office directory of 1861 as a woollen manufacturer and again in 1867. It would appear that she attempted to carry on the business after her husband's death with her nephew, Job Peace though by 1874 whatever was left of their business went into liquidation.

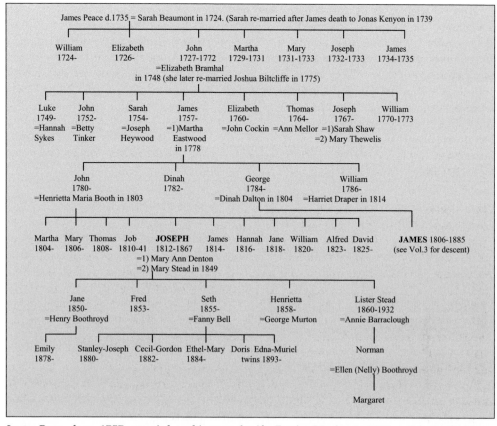

James Peace, born 1757, married, as his second wife, Eunice Mosley in 1792 and had a family.

1899 – 25 February – Huddersfield Weekly Examiner – Supplement

Death of Tedbar Wood.

This gentleman died at Eccles, near Manchester on Friday last week, after a long and painful illness. Mr Wood was a native of Denby Dale, but he and his brother, Benjamin, emigrated, when young men, to Australia, and after amassing considerable fortune, returned to Denby Dale and lived a retired life. Their father and his brothers were at one time, fancy manufacturers in a large way at Denby Dale, but failed in business and Messrs. T & B Wood, afterwards paid the creditors their father's portion in full, with interest. Both they and their immediate ancestors were devoted Wesleyan's and very generous supporters of Denby Dale chapel. They were also very anxious to have a Wesleyan Sunday school with a large hall attached, built in Denby Dale, and when Mr Benjamin Wood died he left £400 towards that object but unfortunately the money was allowed to remain in an Australian bank, and owing to the 'smash' some years ago, both principal and interest (about £700) was nearly all lost. Mr Tedbar Wood also gave a portion of the chapel field (which cost him £260) for the building site, but although the project has not been allowed to entirely die out, it has been considerably delayed.

At the chapel on Sunday the rostrum was draped in mourning and the Rev. S Adcock touchingly referred to Mr Wood's death, and the following hymns were sung in memoriam–

'There is a land of pure delight', 'Where Saints immortal reign', 'Father I know that all my life is portioned out for me', and 'Give me the wings of faith to rise within the veil and see'.

The remains of Mr Wood were interred at St. Nicholas' church, Cumberworth on Tuesday and a large number of sympathising friends attended the funeral.

1914–1919 – Denby Dale and Cumberworth War Memorial

Front panel:– The Great War, 1914 to 1919.

Left panel, 1914–1918:

Mark Atkin	John Eaden Cook
Ralph Armfield	Clifford T S Cunningham
Gladstone Beever	Harry Ellis
George Clement Boothroyd	Keble Thomas Evenett
Frank Eaden Cook	Arthur England
	Jonathan England

Centre panel, 1914–1918

Fred Firth	Arthur Firth
George Edward Gibson	George N Hoyland
Thomas Hodge	Charles G Hinchliffe
Ben Howar	Jos Hirst
Willie Heeley	Herbert Norton Jackson
Edwin Jackson	Harry Kaye
Charles Edward Jelfs	Tom G Littlewood
Thompson Lockwood	James Willie Peace
James Moore	John Pitchfork
Stanley Peace	Archie Roberts
C T William Rigby	Joseph Bottomley Rotherforth

Right panel, 1914–1918

Harry Sheard	John Walshaw
Willie Schofield	Hildred Woodhouse
Ernest Thackra	Arthur Williamson
Willie Wilcock	Clarence Widdowson
Joseph Womersley	John W Wright
Frank Wray	

Centre panel, bottom, 1939–1945

Walter G Alexander	Newell Ellis
Roy Hargrave	John Hirst
Alfred Horsley	Donald Mudd
Frank W Peace	John D Schofield
Cyril Schofield	Ivor Shodbrook
Gilbert Stringer	

1926 – 31 March – Denby & Cumberworth Nursing Association.
The following details are taken from a balance sheet dated 31st March 1926:
President – Mrs Beatrice Wilby
Vice President – Mrs Jonas Kenyon

Committee:

Dr. Archibald	Mrs F J Miller
Dr. Bleasdell (Hon. Mem.)	Mrs Jas. Moore
Mrs Freda Crossland	Mrs Naylor
Mrs. H Hampshire	Mrs Scott
Miss Hinchliffe	Mrs C Senior
Miss Irving	Mrs F Wilkinson
Mrs Jelfs	Miss Wilkinson
Mrs Wm. Longley	

Members of Finance Committee:
Messrs. Job Hollingworth and J R Waldie
Hon. Secretary – Miss Bransgrove
Hon. Treasurer – Mr Walter Kenyon

The organisation was founded in 1923. During 1926 nurses made 4410 visits (an increase of 700 on the previous year) throughout the district. They nursed 268 cases and paid 288 visits to the homes of children attending schools in the area, in addition to which they also made periodic visits to the schools in accordance with their arrangement with the West Riding County Council.

   The balance sheet which was audited on 19th April 1926 by William Wood and Charles E Hoyland was as follows:

Receipts	£	s	d	Payments	£	s	d
Grants:				Nurses salaries and expenses	362	14	8
West Riding County Council	55	0	0	Equipment	6	16	8
Huddersfield Board of Guardians	2	2	0	Workmens compensation insur.		15	0
Denby & Cumb. Urban Dist. Council	15	0	0	National Health Insurance	4	0	2
Gunthwaite & Ingbirchworth Urban District Council	2	0	0	Stationary, printing, & c.	1	19	6
Members Subscriptions	170	19	3	Payment to Nurse under rule 13		5	8
Payments for Nurses services	55	9	9	Sundry items:			
Proceeds from social events:				Postages, Hire of Rooms, & c.	3	11	0
Summer Carnival	88	17	4				
Whist Drives & Dances	73	8	5		380	2	8
Special (Rule 13) Donations	1	2	6	Investment made:			
Bank Interest	5	17	3	£200 War stock, 5%, 1929–1947 at cost	199	17	6
National Health Insurance:							
Nurses contributions	1	16	0	Cash in hand and at Bank	173	12	5
	471	12	6				
Balance in hand from last year	282	0	1				
	753	12	7		753	12	7

Ingbirchworth

1852 – Extract from 'A Gazetteer of Sheffield & District' by William White

Ingbirchworth – a village of 393 inhabitants and 820 acres, chiefly the property of the Earl of Scarborough; Benj. Beever kept the Rose and Crown; Jn. Hanwell was blacksmith; Jn. Holmes was wheelwright; Jn. Jackson was shoemaker, Jonathan Roebuck kept the Travellers Inn; Keturah Wrigley was Toll Collector; the farmers are – Joshua Biltcliffe, Th. Crookes, Jthn. Greaves, Jn. Haigh, Benj. Hallett, Burton and Francis Horn, Wm. Jackson, Chas. Knowles, Th. Wood, J Hanson and Chas. Webster was at Thanet Royd; Chas Knowles also drives a carrier's wagon every Friday from the Sheffield 'Yellow Lion' to Penistone, Ingbirchworth and Denby.

1869 – 2 January – Barnsley Local Board of Health
The Erection of Bridges at Ingbirchworth

As stated at an earlier stage in the proceedings, the Waterworks Committee had agreed to recommend that £50 be contributed towards the cost of two new bridges at Ingbirchworth. This recommendation was the result of an application by the Ingbirchworth Board of Health.

Mr Carter stated at some length, in answer to Mr Taylor, the circumstances, which had induced the committee to make this recommendation. It was necessary for the board that their should be one bridge, but this bridge was not sufficient for the accommodation of the inhabitants of the village, who live on both sides of the stream, and hence it was found that two bridges would be required. The cost of constructing these bridges, which would amount to £110 to £120 for each, was to be raised by subscription. The committee thought that the deputation which waited upon them had made out a good case, and the Board, being the largest rate payer in the township, they decided to recommend that £50 be granted.

1869 – 10 July – Liberal Meeting at Rose and Crown Inn, Ingbirchworth
... prepared by Mr and Mrs Holmes (landlord and lady) .....they engaged the Denby and Denby Dale celebrated brass band.

(This is the earliest mention, so far, for the Denby Dale Brass Band)

1869 – 11 September – An Ingbirchworth Farmer's Son Charged with Sheep Stealing
Edward Taylor, son of Thomas Taylor, farmer of Spicer House, Ingbirchworth was charged with stealing 3 sheep and a lamb from Ambrose Dronfield, a farmer of Hollin Clough, Derwent. Dronfield missed the stock on 16th June and eventually found one his sheep at Denby at the farm of Henry Brooke.

PC Joseph Simpson stationed at Denby, after visiting Brooke's farm and a skin yard in Wath charged Taylor with the theft and locked him up. He was committed to trial to the Derby October sessions, bail being accepted for his appearance himself in £50, his father and another person in £25 each.

Upper & Lower Denby, Birdsedge & Gunthwaite

1344

By John, Abbott of Roche, to Adam de Heley, of Birton, Henry de Seyvile and William de Heley, of the wardship and marriage of William, son and heir of William de Ryley.

Witnesses: Sir John de Bell Monte, knight, **Emery (Aymer) Burdet, Lord of Denby**, and others.

With regard to the Elland Feud documented within Denby & District III, the following has recently come to light. Though it adds substance to the truth behind the legend it also confirms that the Lord of Denby was more than fully aware of the proceedings and was directly involved in the case.

1351 – 6th July

Commission to William de Plumpton, Brian de Thornhill, William de Skarghill, Nicholas de Wortelay, Henry de Sothill, John de Calverlay, Thomas Flemmyng, Robert de Staynton, Adam de Hopton, John Tours, **Aymer Burdet***, William de Mirfield, John de Sheffield, William de Lewenthorpe, William de Beston and Thomas de Fenton, reciting that Adam Beaumond, William de Lockwode and very many other felons indicted of the death of John de Eland, one of the King's Justices appointed to hear and determine trespasses in the West Riding, Co York, gathering to themselves a very great number of felons and evil doers have killed John, son of the said John, because he was suing before the King to punish them for his father's death, and many others of the household and friendship of the said John de Eland, and have committed various assaults on the King's Justices, appointed to hear and determine such homicides, felonies, trespasses and misdeeds, and killed some of their men and servants, and now strive to the utmost of their power to hinder those who indict them, the Justices, the Sheriff and other ministers of the King from executing his mandates and their offices, openly threatening them, and so to hinder if they can, the King from ruling and doing Justice to the people; and appointing them to take the said felons and such others as the Justices shall furnish names of, and bring them to the gaol at York. Wherefore the King commands them on pain of life and limb and all that they can forfeit, to be diligent in the execution of the premises.*
  (Calendar of Patent Rolls, 1350–1354)

A further document dated 1353 mentions Robert del Bothe of Holmfirth, his brother, Richard, Mathew de Hepworth of Huddersfield, Thomas Lister of Almondbury and Ralph de Skelmanthorpe, amongst others. The men were accused of sheltering and harbouring William de Lockwod and Adam Beaumond in the knowledge that the pair were outlaws. The accused were brought before Miles de Stapleton, Sheriff of Yorkshire where they all pleaded not guilty. The twelve jurors upheld their plea and all were acquitted.

1675

Thomas Clarke (Vicar of Huddersfield 1675–1696).

He was the first of two vicars who bore that surname and was presented to the Vicarage on 9th March 1675 by John Ramsden, Esq. (afterwards the first Baronet).

The Vicar was the son of the Rev. Daniel Clarke, MA of King's College, Cambridge, Vicar of Kirkburton, 1642–1649, by his wife, Elizabeth, the daughter of George Burdett of Denby. Daniel Clarke fled the country in 1649 and was described as a 'painful' (painstaking) preacher in the Parliamentary enquiry of 1651.

Thomas was baptised at Kirkburton in 1649. He was the third pluralist Vicar of Huddersfield, as he was also appointed the Rector of Kirkheaton, 1694–1707. Mr Clarke was not popular in Huddersfield, the Rev. Robert Meeke, the incumbent of Slaithwaite, tells us in his diary that on the 10th January, 1693:

I went today with the churchwarden through a great part of our town on behalf of our Vicar who desired me to present a certificate to his parishioners wishing them to certify for him that he hath been a man of sober and peaceful life, painful (i.e.painstaking) in the Ministry. I showed it accordingly to his desire, but very few signed it – a few inferiors. I should be sorry to stand in need of such a certificate, through variance with any, but I should be much more sorry to stand in need and be denied.

Meeke also makes mention of the marriage of Clarke's daughter to Mr Empson in his diary dated, 3rd February 1689:

About 10 o'clock their came a neighbour to desire me to go to his house to meet our Vicar. I went and met him and some other friends, who were come to the marriage of Mr Clarke's daughter. We went to the chapel (Slaithwaite?). Mr Clarke himself joined in marriage his daughter and Mr Empson. From the chapel we went to Huddersfield; dined there. Stayed at the Vicarage all night.

Meeke's diary also relates the following dated 1st May 1694:

Meeke tells us that he went to the Visitation at Wakefield, returned with Mr Clarke and spent the night at Kirkheaton parsonage. The Rev. Oliver Heywood did not give the Rev. Thomas Clarke a particularly good name. In 'his' diary he wrote:–

Mr Clarke, Vicar of Huddersfield, hath behaved himself with strange insolency since he came thither in many things, particularly concerning a house and land worth £10 a year, given to the poor decayed housekeepers of Huthersfield, but he would needs have it in his hands that he might give it to the common poor of the parish, whereby he lost the favour of the townsmen, with many other strange acts. He hath made a law that if any weddings come to church after the clock had struck twelve, the must pay five shillings or not be married.

It may have been this episode which caused Mr Clarke to get up the petition mentioned previously.

Mr Clarke married one Elizabeth Smith who died in 1707 and was buried at Kirkheaton. By her he had five children, one son and four daughters all of whom were baptised at the Huddersfield Parish Church, they were:

(1) Daniel – who was a sugar planter and sugar merchant, for whom his father wrote the following letter:

> *October ye 26th, 1691*
>
> *Cousin Burdett*
>
> *I must beg one kindnesse of you upon ye account of my son Daniele yt (=that) you will step to the Sugar house as soon as you receive this and get him samples of all yor sorts of Sugar at ye lowest prices and witt upon ye backe of each paper and send you by carrier as also ye price of Treackle.*
>
> *Your affect. Kin and Servt.*
>
> *Thomas Clarke*

Daniel Clarke migrated to America; he inherited his father's estate at Ingbirchworth on condition that he returned to England within two years after his mother's death.

(2) Frances, who married Gregory Empson of Wyke. This is the marriage referred to latterly in Meeke's diary.
(3) Elizabeth, married at Kirkheaton in 1682, the Rev. Simon Jenkinson, Vicar of Flintham. After his death she married Mr Clayton who is said to have succeeded Mr Jenkinson at Flintham.
(4) Mary, who married Michael Syddall.
(5) Ann, who married Nicholas Aspinall, her father's curate at Kirkheaton.

By his will proved at York in 1707/8, the Rev. Thomas Clarke bequeathed to the parishes of Huddersfield and Kirkheaton the sum of £20:

> *to be laid out in lands and put out of interest as the Ministers and Chief Inhabitants of the said parishes do think most fit, the income of which to be distributed amongst the poor of the said Parishes that are industrious and yet needful, but constant frequenters of the Church, yearly and every year upon the Feast of St. Thomas the Apostle.*

Apparently, Mr Clarke wished to make amends for the accusations levied against him, but, unfortunately a portion of this charity was merged into the Armitage charity

1682 – Popish Recusants

Thomas Cowper of Knottingley, a Quaker, indicted for being at an unlawful conventickle, contemptuously refused to plead to the indictment, fyned tenn pound, which he refused to pay; to be conveyed to be imprisoned. Barnsley, October 1682.

Joseph Bailey of Denby, Edward Dickinson of the same, Robt Ellis of Penniston and Thos Cowper of Knotingley, Quakers, for absence from church three Sondayes, refused to find sureties: committed to jail.

Joshua Green of Denby, Mathew Burdett of Nether Denby, Thomas Spavald of Bawtrey, William Hill of Thorne, indicted and convicted upon a Premmunire refused to take the oath of allegiance. Committed to jail. Barnsley, October, 1682.

1748 – An Act for Burying in Woollen only.

By way of encouraging the manufacturing of British woollen goods the above act was passed in 1678 by King Charles II, this made it illegal to be buried in any other *'shirt, shift, sheet or shroud'*. The authorities were keen to ensure compliance and certificates were required to be filled in by a witness as proof.

> *I Rachel Helewell, living near Highflatts, in the Parish of Penistone, makes oath that Edward, the son of Edward Dickinson, of Highflatts, abovesaid, deceased, was not wrapped up, wounded or buried in any shift, sheet or shroud, made or mingled with flax, hemp, silk, hair or gold, or silver, or other than what is made of sheep's wool only, nor in any coffin, lin'd or fac'd with any cloth, stuff, or any other thing whatsoever made or mingled with flax, hemp, silk, hair, gold, silver or any other material contrary to the late Act of Parliament for burying in woollen, the 7th day of August 1748.*

> *I, William Hodgson, curate of Cumberworth, do hereby certifie that the day and year abovesaid, the said Rachel Healewell came before me and made such affadavit as above mentioned, according the said late Act of Parliament.*

1852 – Extracts from 'A Gazetteer of Sheffield & District' by William White

Denby – Th. Moorhouse on Mondays, Wednesdays and Fridays drives a carrier's wagon from Snighill, Sheffield to Denby and Huddersfield: there are 3 trains a day from Denby and Cumb. Station to Huddersfield and Sheffield; G. Micklethwaite is carrier every Wednesday from Barnsley 'White Bear' to Denby; William Graham is Parish Constable and farmer.

Gunthwaite – is a township of scattered farms with 77 inhabitants and 1080 acres, A. Bosville being the Lord of the Manor; the farmers are – Jn. Burgin the miller, Benj. and James Holmes at the Hall farms, Joseph and Richard Mills (Milnes) at Broad Oak, Nath. Priest at Burntcote, G Bron, Rachel Fisher, Ingham Milnes, George & Jn. Wood.

1869 – 23 January – Obstructing the Police at Denby

John Burdett was charged with obstructing the police at Denby on the 9th inst. Fined 5s and 7s costs.

1869 – 13 February – Assaulting the Police at Denby

Wm. Beaumont, a powerful looking man, was charged with assaulting police constable Simpson, who is stationed at Denby. The defendant, who was drunk on Tuesday night, was creating a disturbance at the George Inn, Denby, when the police officer was called to eject him. Prisoner struck him several times on the breast and head, but with great difficulty the constable got him handcuffed and took him to Scissett. Another charge was preferred against him by an old woman, 67 years of age, named Mary Hall, living at Denby. The assault complained of took place at the George Inn, on Tuesday afternoon, when the defendant, without any provocation, struck the poor old woman over the eye, which bled freely. The bench committed the defendant to Wakefield House of Correction for two months, being one month for each offence.

1869 – 6 March – Assault at Denby

Enoch Taylor was charged with assaulting Emma Johnson, a young woman, at Denby on the 21st ult. Mr Freeman appeared for the defence. Complainant stated that she is the daughter of George Johnson, landlord of the Junction Inn, Denby. On the evening of the 21st inst. defendant, with two other young men entered her father's house and called for a pint of beer. This was supplied and defendant afterwards began using abusive language. He said he would fight anyone in the room, and among other boasts, declared he could knock anyone's head off. In consequence of this and other acts of misconduct, complainant and her father turned him out. After he had been got outside, he turned round and deliberately struck her, knocking her down. Complainant's father gave corroborative evidence. The defence was that complainant, if struck at all, was struck accidentally, and that the disturbance in the house was created by a person named Taylor. Defendant was fined 20s and costs.

1869 – 3 April – Denby – Appointment of Church Wardens
The appointment of churchwardens for this parish, according to the usual custom, took place on Tuesday last. After a vote of thanks to the wardens – Mr John Micklethwaite, stone merchant, Denby; and Mr B Holmes, of Gunthwaite – for their services during the past year, they were unanimously re-elected for the current year.

1869 – 15 May – One of the Results of the Opening of Gunthwaite Spa.
Enoch Taylor, landlord of the George Inn, Denby, was charged with having his house open on Sunday, the 2nd May at an improper hour. Police Constable Simpson said on the day named he visited the defendant's house at half past four o'clock in the afternoon when he found 18 men in the kitchen, some of whom he knew very well. There were two tables filled with glasses. He called the attention of the landlord to the state of his house, when he said they were all travellers. Witness then pointed out a man he knew very well and who lived at Bursidge which was about three-quarters of a mile off. He went away, and, in company with police constable Goodison, returned again shortly before five o'clock. They found ten men in the kitchen, some of whom were under the influence of drink. Some of the men were the same who were in the house when he first visited it. He went into the parlour and found fifteen men. One man was very drunk. Witness again drew the landlord's attention to the state of the house when he replied; '*The church has loosed*'. The defendant then shouted to his niece and asked her if the church had not loosed and if it was not five o'clock. She replied that it had and that it was five o'clock. The defendant, at some length, cross-examined the witness, with a view to show that all the men who were in the house came from a distance, and came under the designation of 'travellers'. Police constable Goodison corroborated the evidence given by the former witness. The defendant said that the 2nd of May was the day on which the Gunthwaite Spa was opened and there was a large company of people who wanted refreshment. He let in all persons who said they came from a distance, and turned those out who lived in the villages around. Allen Taylor and Jane Norton were called to show that it was turned five o'clock when the men went into the house. The defendant said that he had kept a beer-house and an old licensed house for 17 years, and this was the first time that he had been before a court. The bench said that, as it was the opening day, they would only fine him 10s and costs – in all £1 4s 6d.

1869 – 29 May – Serious Accident to a Denby Gentleman at Barnsley
On Thursday evening a serious accident occurred at Barnsley to Mr Rusby, of Denby. It appears that he had been at Barnsley on business and was returning home on horseback, about six o'clock. When he got on the Cockerham Road the horse he was riding became

restive and threw its rider who fell with his head on the kerb stone by which he received a serious scalp wound. He was removed to the Dispensary where, on enquiry yesterday, we learn he his progressing favourably. It is thought that his brain is not injured, and that with a few days quiet he will be able to be removed to his home. Mr Rusby is connected to the new waterworks at Ingbirchworth.

1869 – 5 June – Serious Case of Wilful Damage at Denby – Heavy Fine

William Beaumont, William Fretwell and John Burdett were charged with doing wilful damage to a quantity of gooseberry, currant and other trees in a garden belonging to Mr Enoch Taylor, George Inn, Denby, to the amount of £1 19s. Mr Hamer appeared for the prosecution and Mr Freeman for the defence. The complainant said he closed his house at eleven o'clock at night but he did not go to bed as he had a horse ill. About two o'clock, he and his son had occasion to go into the stable to look at the horse. He went up into the hayloft to put some hay into the rack, and whilst he was there he heard a noise in the garden. He opened the barn door, which led into the garden, when he found a wheelbarrow with a quantity of shrubs in it. He went into the garden and saw Fretwell, whom he touched on the back. He also saw Beaumont against a wall. There was another man whom at first he could not make out as he had his billycock pulled over his face. He (complainant) however, was about to get over the wall when the man, who had a stick said 'If thou comes over here, damn thee, I will knock thy head off. As soon as the man spoke he knew the voice as that of Burdett. He was in the garden at twelve o'clock the same night when all was right. He then went and called his wife, daughter and son up and he went to the road in front of his house. He saw Fretwell and Burdett go into the house where the former lodged. He also saw Burdett come out of the house with his coat turned inside out. He had known Fretwell and Beaumont ever since they were born and Burdett for the past twenty years. Corroborative evidence having been given by William Taylor and Enoch Taylor, sons of the complainant, and by his daughter, Ann Taylor. Police Constable Simpson said he was on duty on the evening of the 28th ult. when he looked into the Star Inn and saw the defendants Beaumont and Burdett as late as twenty minutes past one o'clock. Arthur Wilby, a valuer, proved being called in to assess the damage done in the garden, which he assessed at £1 19s. Mr Freeman, after delivering a brief address, called Aaron Hanwell, the landlord of the Star Inn, who spoke to Beaumont and Burdett being at his house up to a quarter to three o'clock on the morning of the 28th ult., and were never out. The witness in cross-examination, however, admitted, that they might have been out for a few minutes. Lydia Fretwell, sister to defendant Fretwell, said he went to bed at nine o'clock and was never out again. She swore positively that Burdett was never in her house that night. Witness in cross-examination said she had been at Barnsley and Huddersfield Court Houses before to prove an alibi for her brother. William Wormald, having been called to prove that the complainant was drunk, Mr Superintendent Sykes said he had a long list of offences against Beaumont and Fretwell, but had nothing against Burdett, who it was stated, was the son of a respectable wheelwright. The bench fined Beaumont and Fretwell £5 each and costs, and Burdett £2 and costs, or three months each in default; the damage to be deducted from the fine. Burdett paid the fine at once, but the other two had not done so up to the rising of the court.

1869 – 7 August – A Drunken Row at Denby Dale

Enoch Taylor, William Taylor, Allen Taylor, Oliver Taylor and James Norton were charged by PC Simpson with being drunk and riotous at Denby Dale on Sunday, 11th July. Mr Peacock appeared for the prosecution and Mr Hamer for the defence. The case was a long one but the facts lay in a very small compass. There are two rival public houses at Denby Dale, one of which is kept by the elder Taylor (Enoch). The latter saw the officer about half past twelve o'clock on this Sunday morning and complained that parties had been throwing stones at his door. The officer inspected the door minutely with a light, but could observe only one small mark, which he rubbed off with his finger. As soon as he had done so the whole of the defendants, who were the worse for liquor, commenced to call him a thief, rogue and such like names. Some allusion was made to window breaking, but no one was charged with that offence. The case after a number of witnesses had been examined pro and con, was dismissed.

Breach of Licence

Enoch Taylor, one of the defendants in the above case, was charged with permitting drunk and disorderly conduct in his house. The date of this offence was prior to the last named one. He was fined 5s and costs.

1869 – 14 August – More Midnight Disturbances at Denby

John Micklethwaite, J Norton, Wm. Beaumont and Wm. Fretwell, four respectable inhabitants of Denby, Micklethwaite being a churchwarden, were charged by PC Simpson with being drunk and riotous near the New Inn at one o'clock in the morning of Sunday, July 25th. Mr Hamer appeared for the defence. Beaumont, who did not appear, was ordered to be brought up on a warrant. Micklethwaite had been at the Rose and Crown Inn, Ingbirchworth the previous night, meeting Mr Peacock and several members of the Barnsley Board of Health relative to some business transactions. There was a good deal of conflicting evidence as to the actual condition of the defendants and the magistrates gave them the benefit of the doubt by dismissing the case.

1869 – 11 September – A Farmers Squabble at Denby – Much Ado About Nothing

George Wilby, farmer of Denby, charged Joseph Brooke, residing at the same place, with committing wilful damage to a field of growing grass by taking a reaping machine up the field. The defendant pleaded guilty but said he had the consent of the defendants son, who was 40 years of age, to go up the field. The prosecutor said on the 24th ult. wanted to go up his field with a reaping machine when he refused giving him leave. On the 26th ult., he was near the barn door, when he saw the defendant go up the field with the reaping machine. The defendant admitted the offence, but said as previously stated, that the complainants son gave him leave, or he should not have gone. He had no witnesses, but if the bench would adjourn the case for a fortnight, he could bring a person who had heard the complainant's son give him permission. Mr Kaye, however, advised the parties to settle the case. This was agreed to and the defendant was ordered to pay damage 1s and 13s costs.

1870 – 15 January – Unlawful wounding at Upper Denby

William Taylor (on bail) was indicted for unlawfully and maliciously wounding George Beaumont at Upper Denby, near Barnsley on the 4th December. Mr Barker prosecuted and

Mr V Blackburn defended. The prosecutor is a farm labourer at Upper Denby. On the afternoon of the 4th December he and a man named Fretwell were in Beaumont's mother's stable. As they were there the prisoner and several of his brothers came into the stable, and a quarrel ensued between Fretwell and one of them. In the course of the quarrel Beaumont endeavoured to step between Fretwell and the man with whom he was quarrelling. The prisoner then came behind him and deliberately stabbed him in the thigh. In the course of the case, acting under the advice of his counsel, the prisoner said he would plead guilty to a common assault. Mr Barker consented to this plea being accepted, and the prisoner was sentenced to three months hard labour.

1870 – 26 February – Vagrancy at Denby
Wm. Powell and William Young were charged under the Vagrant Act with being found for an unlawful purpose in an enclosed place at Denby, on Sunday last. It appeared that on the day named, a young lad went into Mr C Rusby's steam saw mill where he found the two prisoners in the fire hole. On the previous evening the place was locked up and all was safe, but shortly after the prisoners left it was found that a pair of leather leggings had been stolen. Information was given to the police, and the prisoners were apprehended at Penistone, but nothing was found upon them. They were committed for fifteen days each to Wakefield, with hard labour.

1870 – 16 April – Match at Stocksbridge – Victory for the Denby shooter
Upwards of 400 persons were present in a field adjoining the house of Mr E Askew, Coach and Horses, Stocksbridge on Saturday, pigeon shooting being the attraction. The contending parties were Mr E Hanwell of Denby and Mr J Bailey of Stocksbridge. The match was for £10 a side, 12 birds each, 1oz. of shot, 21 yards rise, and 60 yards fall. Bailey was the most fancied, still only even money was taken on the match, whilst 5 to 4 was freely laid on the gun. Hanwell won, killing 7 to Bailey 5.

1870 – 16 April – Death by falling down stairs at Denby
A widow woman, named Rebecca Turton, aged 80 years residing at Denby, died on Thursday from the injuries which she received by falling down stairs on the 8th inst. It appears that on the above day deceased slipped her foot and fell down part of the stairs, sustaining a severe fracture on the head. She was attended by Mr Dowse, surgeon, but her injuries were of such a severe nature that she died as above stated.

1870 – 14 May – Abolition of the Tolls on the Huddersfield and Penistone Turnpike Roads
A few days ago the toll gates, houses and c., on the Huddersfield and Penistone turnpike road were put up by auction at the house of Mr Holmes, the Old Crown Inn, Penistone, in consequence of the trust in connection with the above road expiring on the 1st of June next. We understand that the bar house at Penistone bridge and at High Flatts, will in a short time be totally removed.

1870 – 28 May – Alleged Assault at Denby
Jonathan Jackson charged John James Chappell with assaulting him on the 10th inst. at Denby. Both the parties work at one place and the assault arose out of a dispute of no very

grave importance. The defendant, it was alleged, struck at the complainant with a thick piece of wood called a 'stag' and then took him by the whiskers and shook him. Witnesses having being called on both sides the bench considered the case ought never to have come before them and subsequently dismissed it.

Historical Notes taken from
HISTORY OF PENISTONE
By John N Dransfield 1906

Page 14

Hic requiescit pars terrena GULIELMI NORRIS, capellae de Denby nuper ministri; cujus morientis beneficia extento aevo perduci voluerunt hearedes. Ob. 4th Martii, 1733, aet. 74.

Page 59

Wortley Union, first meeting 1838.
Guardian for Ingbirchworth – Mr James Stafford

Page 60

In 1849 Penistone Union was formed.
Guardian for Ingbirchworth – James Stafford
Guardian for Denby – Herbert Camm Dickinson and Joseph Haigh
Guardian for Gunthwaite – James Holmes

Page 60–64

Extracts from old estate books of the Bosville's of Gunthwaite Hall.
Mr Bosville died 6th June 1724 aged 41 and was buried at Penistone. His widow, Mrs Bridget Bosville, married Mr Hugh Bosville as her second husband at Midhope Chapel, 29th Sept 1729.

1726 February 18. To paid purchase money for Broad Oak Farm to Mr Stocks £1200.00.

1729 To paid Mr Allott for eight months serving the cure of Denby Chapell (viz.) from ye 6th January to the 8th September. £16 13s 4d.

1730 To paid Mr Jona. Parkin his salary as curate of Denby Chapell from the 8th September when Mr Allott left to ye 10th December 1729.

1731–2 To received of John Horn in satisfaction for mulcture taken for wheat and meal, ground at his mills for the use of Gunthwaite Hall, which by a covenant of his lease of the mills were to be mulcture free £3 3s.
   Also – to paid the charges of building the house at Gunthwaite Mill £15 17s.

1732–3 To paid in part for erecting 13 seats in Denby Chapell £1 11s 2d

1830 June 9th By paid James Holmes and Thomas Haigh jun. Overseers of the Poor of Denby in the parish of Penistone £10 in lieu of the Right Hon. Lord Macdonald taking a parish apprentice for said Lord Macdonald's woods and plantations in Denby aforesaid, as paid James Holmes and Thomas Haigh jun. Receipt.

1830 November 17th. By paid Rev. Brice Bronwin £12 10s, being for half a year's salary due to him as curate of Denby Chapel in the parish of Penistone the 24th June last.

Page 84
From Oliver Heywood's register:
Daniel Rich, of Penistone Parish, Uncle to Sylvanus Rich of Bullhouse died 1st October 1697, aged 76.

Mr Crook, a Nonconformist Minister, formerly at Denby, lived long in Wakefield, died of the gout in his throat, 9th January 1687, aged 53.

Major Sedascue, a lord's son in Germany, fled into England, 1640; an officer in a Parliamentary army, died at Heath Hall, buried at Normanton 4th December 1688, aged 76.

On Thursday 18th March 1875, the estates at High Flatts and Birdsedge in Denby, and Dearn in Fulstone, of Mr Herbert Camm Dickinson's devisees were offered for sale by Mr A E Wilby at the Rose and Crown Hotel, Penistone, in ten lots.

Lot 1 comprised Mill Bank House, situate at High Flatts, now the well known home for inebriate women – and land and buildings adjoining.

Lot 9 was Thread Mill Farm at Birdsedge.

Lot 10, Dearn House Farm near High Flatts.

Page 138
An Association for the Prosecution of Felons.
On 3rd February 1820 the above was formed for the parish of Penistone. The committee consisted of 15 members amongst whom were:

For Denby – Benjamin Haigh and Joshua Dyson
For Gunthwaite – James Hargreave
For Ingbirchworth – John Hobson.

Page 171
Extracts from the Parish Books of Penistone.
1677. Memorandum, that Widow Roebuck was chosen churchwarden (for Denby quarter) and George Shawe, overseer, but that they made an exchange of their offices by mutual consent.

Page 175
One of the old towns books for the Township of Denby contains the names of the Churchwardens from 1636 to 1740 both inclusive; the names of the overseers of the poor from 1636 to 1848, both inclusive; the names of the surveyors of the highways from 1705 to 1853 both inclusive, the names of the Constables from 1705 to 1833 both inclusive. As some of Mr Dransfields ancestors, the Dickinsons are amongst them, I have made a copy of the whole list in one of my books.

In 1670 Widow Hawksworth, of Broad Oak, was churchwarden for Denby quarter and also overseer of the poor for the Township of Denby the same year and in 1730 Mr Bosville was churchwarden for Denby quarter. This would no doubt be Mr Hugh Bosville, who married as her second husband Mrs Bridget Bosville, the mother of Godfrey Bosville, the owner of Gunthwaite who was then a minor.

Page 196

Regarding the Masters of Grammar school at Penistone.
1668 Nathan Staniforth (the man who wrote the Denby petition for the accused witches), who died 24th November 1702.
   1726 The Rev Jonathan Parkin, he died 3rd May 1751.
   1751 The Rev Francis Haigh, he died 15th November 1776.

Page 283

Ingbirchworth Inclosure Act was passed in 1800. The award thereunder is dated 15th December 1813.
   Denby with Clayton West Inclosure Act was passed in 1800. The award thereunder is dated 14th June 1804.
   The Penistone Inclosure Act was passed in 1819. The award thereunder is dated 28th January 1826.

Page 332

With regard to remaining active members of Conservative Committees, one of the few is John Micklethwaite of Denby.
   Those deceased include:
   Henry Knowles of Ingbirchworth
   Herbert Camm Dickinson of High Flatts, Denby.

Page 335

A Rental of Captain Bosville's Estate for Martinmas, 1722

Gunthwaite	£	s	d	Land Tax £	s	d
Francis Ellison	13	7	2	0	9	4½
John Horn	5	17	9	0	3	9
Thomas Walshaw	7	5	0	0	4	6
Timothy France	1	13	9	0	0	0
John Lockwood	9	3	8½	0	6	13
John Rich	1	7	6	0	0	10½
William Gaunt	13	15	6	0	8	1
John Kilner	9	5	6	0	6	6
Joseph Archer	2	7	6	0	1	6
Widow Micklethwaite	2	0	0	0	1	3
TOTAL	66	3	4½	1	19	7

Denby	£	s	d	Land Tax £	s	d
Samuel Micklethwaite	3	10	3	0	2	3
Elihu Dickinson	2	16	3	0	1	10
Henry Marsden	4	5	0	0	2	7
Abraham Wood	7	0	3	0	4	7
Tobyas Mallinson	7	3	6	0	3	11
Tobyas Mallinson and for Wood					5	
Tobyas Mallinson and for New House				0	0	11
Jonathan Gaunt	3	2	9	0	2	0
Joseph Gaunt	6	16	1	0	4	6
John Robinson	0	5	0	0	0	0
John Norton	3	4	6	0	1	9
John Ward	2	11	9	0	1	8
Joseph Norton	1	0	3	0	0	7
John Kilner	2	5	3	0	1	9
Joshua Gaunt	3	0	3	0	2	1
Joseph Thewlis	2	0	3	0	1	5
Widow Beaumont	9	9	6	0	5	9
John Horn	11	15	3	0	5	0
TOTAL	70	6	1	2	7	7

Cottage and Chief Rents:
Gunthwaite:
Rebbeccah Brooksbank 1s

Denby:
Joseph Mosley   3s 7¼d
Joseph Thewlis for Masons Land   3s ¼d
Richard Marshal   3½d
Mrs Ann Haigh de Aldermanshead   3½d

Page 340
The Broad Oak Farm was purchased and added to the Gunthwaite estate in 1726.

A lease from Captain Bosville to Mr Abraham Wood – an ancestor of the late Mr John Wood of New House, Denby, estate agent and farmer – dated 31st January 1715, of 15 acres of land in Denby for £14 0s 6d a year, would show the rental to be 8 shillings an acre. Molyneaux Bunny, who in 1749 was buried in Penistone Churchyard was one of the witnesses to this lease.

Page 356
There is a tradition alluded to by Johnson, the antiquary, that Henry VIII was entertained at Bretton Hall, the seat of Sir Thomas Wentworth, in one of his northern progresses made in 1540, and Godfrey Bosville, of Gunthwaite, who married one of the Wentworth family, says

that a bed, having the arms of Wentworth and Dronsfield carved thereon, was made for his reception.

Page 493

Gamekeepers

In 1797 John Crossley was keeper to William Bosville for Middop, alias Midhope and Langsett alias Langside. William Ellis do. do. James Hargreave jun., keeper to William Bosville, Esq, for Gunthwaite. John Weatherhead, keeper to Mr Savile for Thurlstone and Denby cum Ingbirchworth.

(Taken from the Leeds Mercury, 28th October 1797)

Cumberworth

1856 – 19 April – On this day the men employed at the Kirkstyle colliery, Cumberworth, belonging to Ellis and Armitage had a narrow escape of their lives. Thirty men and boys went down the mine in the morning. About 10 o'clock the water from an old working suddenly burst into the pit, filling the place in which the men were working in a few minutes. A rush was at once made for the shaft, and all were rescued except two boys named John Turner Noble of Cumberworth and Allen Peel of Skelmanthorpe.

1870 – 9 April – Refusing to Quit the Crown Inn at Cumberworth
Henry Bradley pleaded guilty to refusing to quit the Crown Inn, Cumberworth on the 25th ultimo. The landlord, John Edward Schoefield, said the defendant went into his house drunk about ten o'clock at night, and, as he refused to quit, he had to send for Sergeant Batty to eject him. Fined 1s and costs. In all 12s or 7 days in default.

1870 – 28 May – Assault at Cumberworth
Albert Exley charged Sidney Robinson with assaulting him on the 25th ult. at Cumberworth. Mr Freeman appeared for the prosecution and Mr Frudd for the defence. The parties, it appeared, were at the Queens Head, when some words passed which led to blows, and the defendant, it was alleged, struck the complainant over the mouth and kicked him. Several witnesses were called on both sides but as the evidence was very conflicting, the bench dismissed the case.

1870 – 9 July – A Cumberworth Peace Breaker
William Woodhead, a young man, was charged, on the information of Hezekiah Tinker, innkeeper, Cumberworth, with being drunk and riotous in his house on the 6th inst. Defendant had failed to appear in answer to a summons, and was now brought upon a warrant. Complainant stated that on the night of 6th June last, defendant came to his house at about half past eight. He was intoxicated. He sat down for a few minutes, then began to quarrel with some parties who were in the house. Complainant turned him out but he returned and the policeman had afterwards to take two of the customers to their own houses. This was not the first time that the defendant had been guilty of such conduct, he had carried it on at intervals for two years. PC Worsley gave corroborative evidence. Defendant alleged that complainant allowed parties to 'lake' in his house at dominoes for pairs of trousers. Fined 10s and cost, in all £1 19s 4d.

1870 – 30 July – Cumberworth Charities
Stone's charity. By indenture, dated 26th Jan. 7 James I (1609/10), Edward Stone conveyed unto Robert Hepworth and his heirs, certain closes in Nether Cumberworth, called the North East end of the Hawcliff Ing, the east end of Hawcliff and two closes inclosed from the common fields called East End, subject to a condition for the yearly payments out of the rents and profits on the Friday before Easter of 33s 4d, viz to the churchwarden of the

parish of Silkstone, for that part of Cumberworth called Cumberworth Half, 20s for and towards the relief of the aged and impotent poor dwelling in Cumberworth Half in the said parish, 6s 8d to the said churchwarden towards the repairing of the chapel of Cumberworth and 6s 8d to the churchwarden chosen for the township of Silkstone for the relief of the most ancient and needy poor people of that township and with power of entry and distress to the churchwardens in default of payment. The annuity of 33s 4d is paid by the proprietors of the land charged and it is applied in the proportions and for the purposes mentioned in the deed.

1870 – 13 August – Suicide at Cumberworth

On Tuesday morning last the body of a man named David Bentley, who resided at Kitchenroyd near Cumberworth, was found suspended by the neck from a curtain rod in his bedroom. Mr Dawes, surgeon, was called in but the man was found to be quite dead. Deceased, who was 49 years of age had an apoplectic fit some time ago, and since that time he had been in a desponding state of mind. On Tuesday an inquest was held on the body before Thomas Taylor, Esq. Coroner at the house of Mrs Ann Birthwaite, the 'Travellers Inn', Cumberworth, when a verdict of 'hanged himself whilst in a state of unsound mind was returned.

Scissett

1862 – 11 June – Charles Senior was killed while fighting with Mathew Woodhead, both of Scissett.

1869 – 16 January – Scissett Conservative Gathering
The Conservative working men of the parish of Scissett dined together at the house of Mr Tippler, of Langleys, on Monday last. The Rev H Newland MA, vicar of Scissett took the chair. There were also present the Rev S Campbell, curate of Skelmanthorpe and several active members of Messrs. Stanhope and Starkey at the late election. Excellent addresses were delivered by the Chairman, Mr A Wilby, Denby Dale, Mr J Bottomley, Mr T Wood and others. The attendance was very numerous, and the meeting, which was very enthusiastic, broke up at a late hour.

1869 – 31 July – Cricket – Scissett Young Albion versus High Hoyland
The Scissett club won easily with eight wickets to fall: High Hoyland 31 all out and 31 all out, Scissett 38 all out and 28 for 2.

1869 – 7 August – Scissett Crown Inn Club versus Cawthorne Victoria (cricket)
The Scissett 'Royal' team proved victorious.

1870 – 2 April – Scissett – Visit of a Circus
On Wednesday (30th March) the 'Royal Amphitheatre and Circus' which was accompanied by Wallet, the 'Queens jester' paid a visit to Scissett and gave two performances in a portable tent.

1870 – 30 July – Sudden Death at Scissett
The other morning, about half past four, Edward Calverley, aged 38 years, a labourer residing at Scissett was found by a man named William Harvey laid dead by the roadside. He had been seen the worse for liquor the previous night and Mr Davies, surgeon of Skelmanthorpe, who examined the body, gives it as his opinion that the cause of death was apoplexy. Under these circumstances no inquest has been deemed necessary.

1914–1918 – Names of the Fallen, during the Great War

Norman Batty	Percy Exley	Archie Roberts
Fred Bean	Fred Firth	Tom Stead
Fred Bell	Donald Jackson	Alfred Tyas
John Bowker	Alfred Lacy	George Vigor
Alfred Craven	Harold Peel	Harold J Whittell
Wilfred Everett	Spencer Race	Arthur Wilson
Ernest Exley	Horace Rhodes	